ENDORSEMENTS

Power to Heal is a moving expression of Randy Clark's lifestyle and calling. He lays out a masterful and practical guide on healing like Jesus. Randy proves by his own experience and through the testimonies of thousands of others that the power to heal is for everyone who loves Jesus. *Power to Heal* is available!

Leif Hetland

Author, *Seeing Through Heaven's Eyes*

For such a time as this! Just as Queen Esther was raised up in a critical time for the people of God, key people such as Randy Clark—a forerunner in the ministry of healing—are leading the restoration of the divine role and release of the supernatural power of God today.

For decades Randy has traveled the earth ministering to the sick with all manner of signs and wonders. He has now given the body of Christ a summary of his life's work in this book, *Power to Heal.* In simple language he presents in step by step fashion, the fundamental keys to unleashing the power of God to heal the sick.

I urge you to read this book carefully and integrate its principles into your daily life. The *Power to Heal* can and should become a normal part of your life.

Joan Hunter

Author, Evangelist

www.joanhunter.org

POWER

to

HEAL

DESTINY IMAGE BOOKS BY RANDY CLARK

The Essential Guide to the Power of the Holy Spirit

POWER

to

HEAL

KEYS TO ACTIVATING
God's Healing Power in Your Life

RANDY CLARK

DESTINY IMAGE® PUBLISHERS, INC.

P.O. Box 310, Shippensburg, PA 17257-0310

"Promoting Inspired Lives."

This book and all other Destiny Image and Destiny Image Fiction books are available at Christian bookstores and distributors worldwide.

Cover design by Prodigy Pixel

For more information on foreign distributors, call 717-532-3040.

Reach us on the Internet: www.destinyimage.com.

ISBN 13 TP: 978-0-7684-0731-0

ISBN 13 eBook: 978-0-7684-0732-7

For Worldwide Distribution, Printed in the U.S.A.

6 7 8 / 19 18 17

CONTENTS

FOREWORD

Randy Clark has written the go-to-guide for healing the sick in his book, *Power to Heal*. There are several things I admire about the approach to divine healing in this volume:

- It is Biblically-based and theologically solid

- It is Christ-centered, not man-focused

- It puts the ministry of healing into the hands of the people

- It deals with some of the tough questions people face (Why didn't the person get healed when I prayed for them?)

- It is written by a practitioner, not a spectator

The last point was very important to me. The Gospel doesn't need sideline spectators giving more theological theories to people; it needs women and men of God, like Randy Clark, whose ministries have been forged through fire of personal experience.

Power to Heal is not spiritual fluff; it is a practical toolbox that will help you, your church, your small group, or your ministry team to start praying for the sick on a regular basis. The more people you pray for, the more people you will see healed and touched by the power of God. However, if you don't step out and start ministering to the sick, you will not see any of the incredible breakthrough that God's Word says is available to you.

Many Christians are becoming more open to the idea of God performing the miraculous and healing sickness. What keeps them from stepping out and actually operating in this ministry is *lack of practical, Biblical information on how to heal the sick*. In *Power to Heal*, you will get educated and activated for everyday healing ministry.

People may look at Randy Clark and the international impact his ministry, Global Awakening, is presently having, and mistakenly list him among the "Christian celebrities." This should not be. To know Randy Clark's story, you quickly discover that there have been many, many heartbreaking disappointments along the way. There have been many risks. There have been seasons of great trial and testing. In short, Randy is not a spiritual celebrity; he is an everyday Christ-follower that God has raised up to help other Christ-followers start healing the sick.

And with *Power to Heal*, you will see that healing and miracles are not the end goal—they are the means through which Jesus is advancing His Kingdom on Earth and bringing people to salvation!

If you want to start praying for the sick and experiencing Biblical results, I strongly recommend you read *Power to Heal* with an open mind and a heart of expectation!

Chauncey W. Crandall IV, M.D.
Cardiologist
Author of the bestselling books,
Raising the Dead and *Touching Heaven*

INTRODUCTION

Would you like to activate God's healing power in your life? Would you like to be used by God to heal others? God wants to use you. Jesus himself gave us the mandate to heal in the Great Commission when He said,

> *Go therefore and make disciples of all the nations, baptizing them in the name of the Father and of the Son and of the Holy Spirit, teaching them to observe all things that I have commanded you* (Matthew 28:19-20).

I believe that God intended the ministry of healing to be a matter of great importance in the life of all believers, not a side issue. Jesus wants us to be disciples who embrace everything He commanded us to do, not to pick and choose. When you study the gospels and survey the early church, you will see that healing was a normative part of the life of the early church, not some unusual practice relegated to the few and the holy. Jesus is to be our model in all things. He healed the sick and we need to follow His model.

The ministry of healing is basic Christina discipleship. I consider it Discipleship 101. Unfortunately, the ministry of healing has been lost for much of the church. Some believe healing is not for today; that is ceased with the establishment of the early church. Others believe in healing but are not confident that God can or will use them to heal the sick. Neither of these is true. Healing is for the church today, and God will use you to heal. This is the truth of the gospel.

In the pages ahead I want to help you break down the barriers to healing that have been erected in your life and give you practical, biblical teaching on how you can reclaim the power to heal the sick. My prayer is that healing will once again become the norm in the 21st century church and in your life, and the life of every believer. It is my great desire to help every Christian learn to walk in the supernatural power of the Holy Spirit, as a normal part of daily life, exercising *all* of the gifts given to believers.

As we begin this study together, I want to give you a solid biblical foundation for the ministry of divine healing, using Scripture to show you how easy it is to release God's power to heal. If you consider yourself a follower and disciple of Jesus, you are already qualified to walk in God's healing power. It really is that simple. God can use *you* to release His healing power and change the world around you, but it all starts with figuring out what you believe about your qualifications to carry His power. Healing ministry is not reserved for the spiritually elite. It was not exclusive to the apostles, disciples, or the early church. You are qualified to be used by God to heal.

God is not the one restraining the church from stepping out in His supernatural power. It is up to us to combat the lie that we are not qualified to heal, and start believing that we have what God says we have! He provides the power. We just need to learn how to partner with Him.

It's important you understand foundational biblical truths about healing. The One who healed in times past still heals today. Scripture is quite clear when it tells us that, *"Jesus Christ is the same yesterday, today, and forever"* (Heb. 13:8). Jesus has commissioned you and I to do the same works that He did while He was physically present on the earth (see John 14:12). In fact, He tells us that we will do even greater works than He did. When Jesus says *greater,* I believe He means that the works we do in His name in the power of the Holy Spirit will be greater in size and scope because He [Jesus] is no longer on the earth restricted to a single human body. He now lives in each one of us. Think of it—Jesus living inside each believer—that is an amazing increase of the presence and power of God on the earth today! Imagine how we could bring the Kingdom of God to bear on this broken and hurting world if every believer understood and operated from a position of Christ within us!

Because of His atoning work on the cross, every single person who places their trust in Jesus becomes eligible to be filled with the Holy Spirit. When Jesus walked the earth, *He alone* carried the presence and person of the Holy Spirit, for Jesus alone was a fit vessel to be filled with the presence of holy God. Holiness could only indwell perfection. The Spirit could not indwell sinful humanity because He needed a compatible vessel in order to take up habitation. This is why Jesus was the only one fit to have the Spirit come upon Him and *remain* (see John 1:33).

Jesus lived a sinless life, died as our substitute, rose from the grave, ascended to heaven, and sent the Holy Spirit. It was only after the work of redemption was finished that He could send the Spirit, because the Spirit needs a righteous place in which to dwell. Jesus' blood makes us righteous, which means we are filled with the Spirit! I repeat: if you have placed your faith in the Lord Jesus Christ as your Savior, and have submitted your life to His lordship, then you are filled with the same power that resided in Jesus that healed the sick, raised the dead, and delivered the oppressed.

When Jesus died on the cross, He made provision for our righteousness. He made it possible for sinful people to positionally become the righteousness of God in Christ Jesus (see 2 Cor. 5:21). Faith in Jesus' atonement transforms our position before God. Previously we were sinners and thus alienated from an intimate, personal relationship with God. As unbelievers we could not carry God's healing power because we could not be vessels for His presence. You and I have no power in and of ourselves. We have no ability to heal. It is only the presence of the Holy Spirit within us that releases God's power through us. God went to extraordinary lengths to make it possible for you and me to be filled with His presence so we could, in turn, release His power to those in need around us.

GOD DOES NOT CALL THE QUALIFIED— HE QUALIFIES THE CALLED

You may not *feel* qualified to be used by God to heal and deliver. You may be thinking of all the reasons you are not qualified to walk in this expression and demonstration of God's power. But the truth is, God is not looking for the perfect. He is looking for the righteous! This is the power of Jesus' blood—that the unrighteous have become righteous in God's sight. You did not qualify yourself to receive the Spirit's presence; God did. If you think you are not qualified to lay your hands on the sick and release God's healing power, you are right. You could not qualify yourself, so God did the job for you through Jesus Christ. He did what you could not do.

Too many Christians today never move beyond the promise of an afterlife in heaven because they are convinced that their pasts, their mistakes, and their failures disqualify them for supernatural service on earth. Are there new levels of anointing and power that you can walk in? Absolutely! Does God call us to live lives that are consecrated, sanctified, and holy? Yes, Scripture makes this abundantly clear. The problem is that some believers are waiting until they are perfect before they step out and take God at His Word *where they are*. This is really a spiritual paradox.

When we step out and pray for the sick, what are we practicing? We are practicing nothing other than obedience to what Jesus commanded. Not only are we becoming channels for God's supernatural power, but we are also cultivating the fruit of the Spirit in our lives. It is not an either-or situation with God. It is not the fruit of the Spirit *or* the gifts of the Spirit; it is not the character of Christ *or* the power of Christ. It's both!

When you respond to God's leading by praying for the sick, you are obediently fulfilling the commission of Jesus. You are bringing the Kingdom of God into a specific situation, and you are yielding to the Spirit's prompting. Do not wait to become qualified before you start walking in God's healing power. Resolve in your heart today that you will step out in obedience and faith. Remember, God does not call the qualified; He qualifies the called! You are called because of who lives inside of you. There is a stewardship you have with the presence and person of the Holy Spirit.

In the pages that follow I am going to show you very practical ways in which you can cooperate with the Holy Spirit in your everyday life so that you can embrace the power to heal. He is after all the one who lives inside of us. Shouldn't we learn how to work with him?

Consider these words from the apostle Paul: *"But we have this treasure in earthen vessels, that the excellence of the power may be of God and not of us"* (2 Cor. 4:7). Believe it or not, God uses your weaknesses and failures to demonstrate that it is His delight to use broken vessels. If you continue to wrestle with the issues of sanctification and holy living as reasons why you are "waiting" for God to use you, remember that stepping out and obediently doing the works of Jesus is a means of sanctification. James tells us to be *doers* of the Word, not merely hearers only (see James 1:22). Jesus makes it abundantly clear that the pathway to sanctification is doing what He says. When we obey what He has told us to do, we are building our lives on the solid rock (see Matt. 6:24-29; 7:24).

We have seven concepts about the power to heal still to examine, but you will not be able to receive and apply their truths until you fully embrace the truth that you are qualified for this kind of supernatural service. By His grace alone you are qualified. God is with you! It is not you who performs the miracle or brings the healing. You are simply a vessel of clay but you *do* carry the presence of the One who can do all things. Nothing is impossible to the Holy Spirit who has taken up residence within you. Live like this is true and you will begin to see God demonstrate His healing power in and through your life in miraculous ways.

PART 1

ACTIVATE

But you shall receive power when the
Holy Spirit has come upon you.
—Acts 1:8

Chapter 1

HEALING AND THE GOSPEL—THEN AND NOW

How do you receive and release God's supernatural power to heal the sick? First, you *do not* need to convince God to use you. He is already set on that. If you are a believer in Jesus Christ, then you are already qualified for the healing ministry. To receive this power, you simply need to believe that the Holy Spirit within you is capable of healing the sick. Your belief does not add to or subtract anything from God's power working in you. The Bible is truth. What we believe is important because it determines how we respond to truth. If we do not believe the Spirit of God within us desires to heal others *through* us, we will not appropriate and release His healing power. It's available. It's within you. You simply need to step out, believe you are anointed, trust that God wants to use you, and start taking risks.

Lack of knowledge is one barrier that keeps many Christians from stepping out in the healing ministry. Either they have been given incorrect information about God's ability or willingness to heal, or they have simply heard *nothing* about it at all. In the pages ahead, I want to lay out the basic essentials of God's healing power and biblically clarify that He still heals today.

IF YOU ARE A BELIEVER IN JESUS CHRIST,
THEN YOU ARE ALREADY QUALIFIED
FOR THE HEALING MINISTRY.

HEALING TODAY

Healing the sick is not a side issue; it is actually a key benefit of the atoning work of Jesus Christ. While He came to forgive our sins and remove the barrier that separated humanity from God, His work on the cross also made provision for our physical healing. We see this prophetically expressed in Isaiah 53:4-5, which speaks of the coming Messiah:

> *Surely He took up our pain and bore our suffering, yet we considered Him punished by God, stricken by Him, and afflicted. But He was pierced for our transgressions, He was crushed for our iniquities; the punishment that brought us peace was on Him, and by His wounds we are healed* (NIV).

HEALING THE SICK IS NOT A SIDE ISSUE;
IT IS ACTUALLY A KEY BENEFIT OF THE
ATONING WORK OF JESUS CHRIST.

Jesus is the Suffering Servant of Isaiah 53 who carries our infirmities and our diseases. This provision for divine healing in the atonement is confirmed later on in Matthew 8:16-17, as Matthew's evidence that Jesus was fulfilling Isaiah 53.

> *When evening came, many who were demon-possessed were brought to Him, and He drove out the spirits with a word and healed all the sick. This was to fulfill what was spoken through the prophet Isaiah: "He took up our infirmities and bore our diseases"* (NIV).

And the apostle Peter confirms it in his epistle, describing the Lord's passion:

> *Who Himself bore our sins in His own body on the tree, that we, having died to sins, might live for righteousness—by whose stripes you were healed* (1 Peter 2:24).

We live in a fallen world that has been stained by sin. This is why we have sickness, disease, and illness. Emotional dysfunction and torment abound because this planet is still under the influence of the prince of the power of the air, who is Satan (see Eph. 2:2). Medical and psychiatric help can benefit many people. In fact, the very practice of medicine in and of itself reveals the healing heart of God. He desires for people to be whole and restored in every area of their lives. Sometimes medical help is slow, unhelpful, and even detrimental. The fact of the matter is that we cannot place our ultimate confidence in medicine, as it is fallible. This is why it is so important for you to learn to release God's power in your life. The world is looking for answers. People are desperate for solutions to their maladies. While we as believers do not claim to have all the answers, we are filled with the Spirit of the One who has all wisdom, power, and healing virtue. Alone we have nothing, but filled with Christ we have everything.

> ALONE WE HAVE NOTHING, BUT FILLED
> WITH CHRIST WE HAVE EVERYTHING.

It is through the atoning work of Jesus that God provides many blessings for the world He so loves. Jesus' victory over the dominion of darkness is absolutely complete. The power of His blood impacts every realm of living—the spirit, soul, and body. For us to truly live in the atonement means we live from a position of absolute victory, which includes freedom over bondage to sin, shame, guilt, demonic oppression, torment, curses, satanic activity, sickness, disease, and emotional illness. This is what the cross has made available to you and to everyone else who receives its fullness. As Christians, we have a wealth of inheritance to draw from. We do not need to twist God's arm to give these things to us; they are freely provided. It's time for us to access everything God makes available to believers, and to start releasing these things to the world around us.

For a more complete understanding of how to access your inheritance in Christ, I encourage you to read *There Is More: The Secret to Experiencing God's Power to Change Your Life.* In its pages you will find a more comprehensive teaching on how you can personally appropriate God's blessings for yourself or have them activated through impartation. Right now, however, I want us to focus on laying a foundation for stepping into the ministry of healing. It's time for you to freely give what you have freely received in Christ. Interestingly enough, the very context of this phrase—"freely received, freely give"—is supernatural ministry. As Jesus was instructing His disciples, He said:

> *And as you go, preach, saying, "The kingdom of heaven is at hand." Heal the sick, cleanse the lepers, raise the dead, cast out demons. Freely you have received, freely give* (Matthew 10:7-8).

In Christ, you have freely received God's supernatural power. Now it's time to activate and freely release what you have received through the atonement.

HEALING AND THE GOSPEL

Some who claim to believe in divine healing are quick to classify it as secondary to the miracle of salvation—the new birth. Of course this is true. There is no greater miracle than a dead heart converted from darkness and translated into the Kingdom of God (see Col. 1:13). However, in our effort to emphasize the priority and pricelessness of salvation, we tend to give healing an improper, subservient role in advancing the gospel.

SUPERNATURAL HEALING IS NOT A SIDE ITEM SEPARATE FROM THE GOSPEL; IT IS PART OF THE GOSPEL OF THE KINGDOM OF GOD.

Recognize that supernatural healing is not a side item separate from the gospel; it is *part* of the gospel of the Kingdom of God. If you have ever heard the term *full gospel*, it usually describes a message that is accompanied by power. Paul made this very clear when he wrote, *"the kingdom of God is not in word but in power"* (1 Cor. 4:20). While there is a verbal element to sharing the gospel, the complete and full presentation of this "message" comes through supernatural demonstration.

Consider once again the words of Paul, who concludes his letter to the church in Rome:

> *For I will not dare to speak of any of those things which Christ has not accomplished through me, in word and deed, to make the Gentiles obedient—in mighty signs and wonders, by the power of the Spirit of God, so that from Jerusalem and round about to Illyricum I have fully preached the gospel of Christ* (Romans 15:18-19).

**WHEN POWER IS RELEASED, THE GOSPEL IS ACTUALLY
PRESENTED IN PROCLAMATION AND DEMONSTRATION.**

To embrace a full or complete gospel is to believe that we have been given more than just teaching or a message. It is to believe that our message is one that is delivered through power. When power is released, the gospel is actually presented in proclamation *and* demonstration. This is why Paul likely used the phrase *"fully preached the gospel of Christ."* He did not simply come with a message comprised of words, oration, and eloquence. The Greeks were quite proficient in delivering swirling words using their stunning oratory skills. As believers, we carry something greater than philosophy or knowledge. God Himself dwells within us and delivers His message to the world using miracles, signs, and wonders. This is the gospel of the Kingdom we are to proclaim.

John the Baptist proclaimed this gospel in the wilderness (see Matt. 3:2). When Jesus arrived on the scene, not only did He continue to preach this gospel but He also demonstrated it. He gave visible expression to what this gospel looked like.

I want to pause here and clarify for those who are wrestling with a gospel-of-the-Kingdom paradigm. This paradigm does not count salvation as merely one blessing among others. Conversion is absolutely pivotal for entry into the Kingdom. Salvation was and is the exclusive means by which someone enters the Kingdom of God. There is no other means of entry into the Kingdom except through believing in the redemptive work of the Lord Jesus Christ. If you are a Christian, you have experienced this incredible spiritual transformation.

As believers, we carry something greater than philosophy or knowledge. God Himself dwells within us.

But here is the problem so many believers face today: You've made Jesus Lord of your life. You have experienced a life-changing conversion. You were translated out of darkness into the family of God. You eagerly anticipate your home in heaven...*one day*. The logical question is, *"What about today?"* We cannot buy into a gospel that works in heaven but not on earth. The gospel is every bit as relevant to us on earth today as it will be in heaven. Jesus did not inaugurate a system that would only become useful after we die or when He returns to earth in the second coming. His atoning work on the cross made it possible for you and me to become vessels of God's power, continuing Jesus' restorative mission on earth *today*.

Chapter 2

JESUS HEALED THE SICK

WHAT WOULD JESUS ACTUALLY DO?

Back in the 1990s, the popular question in the Christian community was, "What would Jesus do?" We must be careful not to limit our answer exclusively to moral character development. To be honest with our answer we must look closely at Scripture. In Acts 10:38, we read *"how God anointed Jesus of Nazareth with the Holy Spirit and with power, who went about doing good and healing all who were oppressed by the devil, for God was with Him."* Like Luke, John also tells us *"the Son of God was manifested, that He might destroy the works of the devil"* (1 John 3:8). One of the ways that Jesus destroyed the works of the devil was to minister divine healing and deliverance to the sick and afflicted. We have been commissioned to continue this ministry of destroying the works of Satan today.

Why was divine healing so important in the life and ministry of Jesus? Consider the following:

- Divine healing was proof that Jesus was the long-awaited Messiah.

- Divine healing was proof that Jesus had authority on earth to forgive sins.

- Divine healing was proof to others that the Kingdom of God was at hand.

- Divine healing was proof of God's love and compassion.

- Divine healing was proof of God's power and authority over disease.

Additionally, miraculous healings were key tools that Jesus used to draw people to Himself. He never meant for this ministry of healing to stop with Him alone. As He was preparing to send out the disciples in John 20, Jesus said, *"As the Father has sent Me, I also send you"* (John 20:21). Essentially, Jesus was telling the disciples, "What the Father sent Me to do, *you* are going to do the same things." This seems to echo His words in John 14:12:

> *Most assuredly, I say to you, he who believes in Me, the works that I do he will do also; and greater works than these he will do, because I go to My Father.*

This commission is available for us today. Not only are we qualified to walk in God's healing power, but we are actually *commissioned* to minister healing to others.

As you read through the four gospels it is abundantly clear that healing the sick was a central part of Jesus' earthly ministry. From the moment He launched His public ministry, healing was a key component because it was His mission. In Luke 4:18, Jesus, citing Isaiah 61, says,

> *The Spirit of the Lord is upon Me, because He has anointed Me to preach the gospel to the poor; He has sent Me to heal the brokenhearted, to proclaim liberty to the captives and recovery of sight to the blind, to set at liberty those who are oppressed.*

He specifically mentions healing the brokenhearted, bringing deliverance to the captives, recovering sight to the blind, and setting the oppressed free. Time after time the gospel writers' descriptions of Jesus placed teaching, healing, and exorcism in the same context (see Matt. 4:23-25) because these things comprised His earthly ministry.

Let's look at what the Bible has to say about why Jesus healed the sick and why He continues to heal today.

#1: BECAUSE HE WAS SENT BY THE FATHER

Jesus was sent by His Father to complete His Father's mission on earth. Several times we see Jesus describing how the Father "sent Him."

> *But I have a greater witness than John's; for the works which the Father has given Me to finish—the very works that I do—bear witness of Me, that the Father has sent Me* (John 5:36).

For I have come down from heaven, not to do My own will, but the will of Him who sent Me (John 6:38).

Then Jesus said to them, "I shall be with you a little while longer, and then I go to Him who sent Me" (John 7:33).

#2: BECAUSE SOMEONE ASKED HIM TO HEAL

Jesus healed in response to those in need. This included the multitudes who were sick, as well as friends and family.

Four instances of particular note are: Jesus healing the centurion's servant (see Matt. 8:5-13), Jesus healing Jairus' daughter (see Mark 5:22-24,35-43), Jesus healing the leper (see Matthew 8:2-3), and Jesus healing the crowds who came to Him as He was preaching (see Luke 4:40).

#3: BECAUSE MIRACLES, SIGNS, AND WONDERS REVEAL THE FATHER

One revelation of God's nature is healing. Since Jesus was sent to show us the Father, it follows that He would do this in part by ministering healing. In the book of Exodus, God reveals Himself as Healer: *"For I am the Lord who heals you"* (Exod. 15:26). This self-revelation confirms that throughout history God's very nature was defined by healing. We also see this in Psalm 103:3, as King David describes God as one *"who forgives all your iniquities, who heals all your diseases."*

By doing the works of God, Jesus gave the world the most accurate picture of who the invisible God is. This is why Paul writes in Colossians 1:15 that *"Christ is the visible image of the invisible God"* (NLT).

The works of Jesus give us a clear view of God's will to bring healing and wholeness to the earth, because the Son only does what He first saw His Father doing.

> *Jesus gave them this answer: "Very truly I tell you, the Son can do nothing by Himself; He can do only what He sees His Father doing, because whatever the Father does the Son also does"* (John 5:19 NIV).

#4: BECAUSE IT PROVED HIS IDENTITY AS THE MESSIAH

Healing offers scriptural proof of Jesus' clear identity as the Messiah. Let's revisit Luke 4:18-19 for a moment. In this passage we see Jesus announce in the synagogue that He has come to heal, deliver, bring liberty, and bind up the brokenhearted. Then he rolls up the scroll and, to the shock of everyone present, He says, *"'Today this Scripture is fulfilled in your hearing'"* (Luke 4:21). Based on what Jesus was quoting from Isaiah 61, the expected Messiah was prophesied to have a healing ministry. Jesus' announcement that He was the fulfillment of Isaiah 61 revealed that He is indeed the Savior sent from God. Is it any wonder His statements caused such stirring controversy among those who were present in the synagogue that day?

Jesus' response to John the Baptist is another instance in which He confirms His Messianic identity. While John was in prison, he sent two of his disciples to Jesus, asking Him, *"Are You the Coming One, or do we look for another?"* (Luke 7:19). *Jesus answered and said to them, "Go and tell John the things you have seen and heard: that the blind see, the lame walk, the lepers are cleansed, the deaf hear, the dead are raised, the poor have the gospel preached to them"* (Luke 7:22).

#5: AS PROOF OF HIS DIVINE AUTHORITY TO FORGIVE SINS

In Mark 2:1-12 and Luke 5:17-26, we find the well-known account of Jesus teaching in a crowded house. Four men carry their paralyzed friend on a stretcher to the place where Jesus is teaching, hoping to get him in front of Jesus because they believe Jesus can heal him. Unable to get to Jesus because of the crowds, they climb onto the roof, remove the tiles, and lower their friend down on ropes. The scripture tells us that Jesus not only healed the man, but He also forgave his sins.

> *When He saw their faith, He said to him, "Man, your sins are forgiven you." And the scribes and the Pharisees began to reason, saying, "Who is this who speaks blasphemies? Who can forgive sins but God alone?"*

But when Jesus perceived their thoughts, He answered and said to them, "Why are you reasoning in your hearts? Which is easier, to say, 'Your sins are forgiven you,' or to say, 'Rise up and walk'? But that you may know that the Son of Man has power on earth to forgive sins"—He said to the man who was paralyzed, "I say to you, arise, take up your bed, and go to your house."

Immediately he rose up before them, took up what he had been lying on, and departed to his own house, glorifying God. And they were all amazed, and they glorified God and were filled with fear, saying, "We have seen strange things today!" (Luke 5:20-26).

JESUS RECOGNIZED THAT THERE WERE TWO
CONFLICTING KINGDOMS AT WAR ON THE EARTH—
THE KINGDOM OF GOD AND THE KINGDOM OF SATAN.

#6: AS PROOF THAT THE KINGDOM OF HEAVEN WAS ON EARTH, AMONG MEN

Jesus recognized that there were two conflicting kingdoms at war on the earth—the Kingdom of God and the kingdom of Satan. As the Kingdom of God advanced on the earth, by default the dominion and works of the enemy were being destroyed (see 1 John 3:8). Practically speaking, God's Kingdom advanced through healing and deliverance, as both were ways that Jesus loosed people from demonic affliction.

In Luke 13, as Jesus was setting a woman free from a spirit of infirmity, He asked the religious synagogue ruler, *"So ought not this woman, being a daughter of Abraham, whom Satan has bound—think of it—for eighteen years, be loosed from this bond on the Sabbath?"* (Luke 13:16). As this woman was healed from the spirit of infirmity, the power of Satan was broken over her life as the Kingdom of God came near to her.

Earlier in Luke 11, people were accusing Jesus of casting out a demon by the power of Beelzebub, the ruler of demons. He explains that it would be illogical for Satan to cast out Satan, as this would bring division to his kingdom. He continues, *"But if I cast out demons with the finger of God, surely the kingdom of God has come upon you"* (Luke 11:20).

Healing and deliverance demonstrate that the Kingdom of God has come near. Jesus announced the emergence of this Kingdom through preaching and demonstrated its arrival by healing the sick and casting out demons. We can do the same today with the power of the One who lives in us—the power of Jesus Christ!

Chapter 3

WHY WE SHOULD
HEAL THE SICK

Now that you have received an overview of why Jesus healed the sick, it is important for you to grasp that His mission is *your* mission. Healing was not exclusive to Jesus' earthly ministry. It continued in the book of Acts, throughout the early church, *and* the expectation is for it to remain a key part of the gospel throughout time immemorial. Since Jesus' mission belongs to you, let's examine the reasons that you, as a Spirit-empowered believer, have also been called to heal the sick.

#1: JESUS IS OUR MODEL

If you believe in Jesus, you are called and empowered to do the same works that He did. This commission comes directly from the words of Jesus. It is not locked into a certain period of history or a specific dispensation; it is the normative expectation of all believers throughout all of time, to do the works of Jesus, which includes healing the sick, among many other things. Most assuredly, I say to you, he who believes in Me, the works that I do he will do also... (John 14:12).

IF YOU BELIEVE IN JESUS, YOU ARE CALLED AND EMPOWERED TO DO THE SAME WORKS THAT HE DID.

#2: GOD USES PEOPLE TO RELEASE THE BLESSINGS OF THE ATONEMENT

Isaiah 53 prophetically confirms that divine healing is provided in the atoning work of Christ. How is this healing power appropriated and released then? Generally, it is released through people like you and me. This is God's plan for a collaborative relationship with humanity. Consider how God collaborates with us. God uses people to preach salvation, to teach sanctification, to exercise spiritual gifts that edify the body of Christ, to bring deliverance from demonic torment, and to break the curses of poverty and hopelessness.

God is almighty and sovereign and is more than capable of doing all of these things by His own supernatural power—and on some occasions, He does. However, God's primary method of operation is to use anointed human beings to carry out His redemptive purposes on the earth.

GOD'S PRIMARY METHOD OF OPERATION
IS TO USE ANOINTED HUMAN BEINGS TO
CARRY OUT HIS REDEMPTIVE PURPOSES.

#3: GOD USES PEOPLE TO RELEASE THE BLESSING OF HEALING

Throughout the Old Testament, most of the recorded healings came about through the physical activity of a prophet or leader. Even under the Old Covenant, people were instrumental vessels for the ministry of healing. Here are a few examples:

1. Moses prayed for Miriam's healing from leprosy (see Num. 12:13).

2. Elisha prayed to raise the widow's son from the dead (see 2 Kings 4:18-37).

3. Elisha sent Naaman to bathe in the Jordan River for his healing (see 2 Kings 5:1-19).

4. Isaiah ordered a poultice for Hezekiah's healing (see 2 Kings 20:1-11).

As we transition into the New Testament, the gospels are full of instances where Jesus directly brought healing, usually with the touch of His hand or through some other physical action, but we also find numerous accounts of healings worked by the Lord through the agency of human beings. Jesus sent His disciples out to preach and heal the sick (see

Matt. 10; Mark 6; Luke 9 and 10). Even though the Holy Spirit had not yet come upon all believers—because Jesus was still on the earth—by commissioning the disciples to preach the Kingdom and heal the sick, Jesus was acclimating them to what would become normative once the Holy Spirit came at Pentecost.

WE ARE THE VEHICLES AND VESSELS GOD WANTS TO USE TO RELEASE HIS DIVINE HEALING POWER.

The book of Acts is filled with examples of believers carrying out Jesus' mission to heal the sick. For instance: Philip healed many in Samaria (see Acts 8:5-7), Ananias healed Paul's eyes (see Acts 9:10-18), Peter healed the lame man at the temple (see Acts 3:1-8), and healed Aeneas at Lydda (see Acts 9:32-35). Peter raised Dorcas from the dead at Joppa (see Acts 9:36-42). Paul raised Eutycus from the dead (see Acts 20:12), and we are told that many extraordinary miracles were done by Paul in Ephesus (see Acts 19:11-12). When we examine the New Testament closely, there are few, if any instances of God healing by His own sovereign power without using a human agent.

If the blessing of divine healing provided in the atoning sufferings of Jesus on the Cross is to be released among God's people and among unbelievers, it is important that we who believe in Jesus are involved in ministering to the sick. We are the vehicles and vessels God wants to use to release His divine healing power.

#4: MINISTRY TO THE SICK DEMONSTRATES GOD'S LOVE AND REVEALS HIS HEART

As we continue the ministry of Jesus here on earth, we recognize that we are called to do what He was anointed to do. Once again, we find this list in Isaiah 61:1-4 and then repeated in Luke 4:18-19, as Jesus defines the purpose for which He was sent. God's heart is to heal the broken-hearted, set captives free, bring sight to the blind, liberate the oppressed, and proclaim the acceptable year of the Lord. All of these things are motivated by God's heart of compassion.

AS WE CONTINUE THE MINISTRY OF JESUS HERE ON EARTH, WE RECOGNIZE THAT WE ARE CALLED TO DO WHAT HE WAS ANOINTED TO DO.

The gospels introduce us to Jesus' heart of compassion in passages like Mathew 14:14: *"When Jesus landed and saw a large crowd, He had compassion on them and healed their sick"* (NIV). When the leper came to Jesus, asking to be healed, we see that, *"moved with compassion, Jesus reached out and touched him. 'I am willing,' He said. 'Be healed!'"* (Mark 1:41 NLT). This instance reveals both God's willingness to heal and His compassion that motivates the healing. In Jesus' statement, *"I am willing,"* we hear a powerful expression of God's heart.

The question then is, "Is healing for *everyone?*" I believe you will discover the answer for yourself in the following passages:

*When evening had come, they brought to Him many who were demon-possessed. And He cast out the spirits with a word, and **healed all** who were sick* (Matthew 8:16).

We see that Jesus healed *all* who were sick. Not some. Not a sovereign select group. He healed *all* who were sick and demonized. Luke describes the same occasion using these words:

*Now when the sun was setting, all those who had anyone sick with various diseases brought them to Him; and **He laid His hands on every one of them and healed them*** (Luke 4:40).

Jesus healed everyone who came to Him for healing. There were no exceptions! In fact, there is no record of anyone who asked Jesus for healing that was denied, even when large crowds pressed upon Him.

IT IS CHRIST'S AUTHORITY IN OPERATION THROUGH US TO HEAL THE SICK AND REVEAL THE SUPREMACY OF GOD'S POWER OVER ALL THINGS.

#5: HEALING THE SICK DEMONSTRATES GOD'S SUPERNATURAL POWER

Jesus holds authority, which is given to Him by the Father, over sickness and disease and demon oppression. When it comes to our role in healing, it is interesting to note that before presenting the Great Commission, Jesus announced, *"All authority has been given to Me in heaven and on earth"* (Matt. 28:18).

Since we are filled with the Spirit of Christ, we have also received the authority of Christ. It is not our authority; it is Christ's authority in operation through us to heal the sick and reveal the supremacy of God's power over all things.

In the gospel accounts, when Jesus commissioned the disciples to go into different towns and preach, He gave them power. *"when He had called His twelve disciples to Him, He gave them power over unclean spirits, to cast them out, and to heal all kinds of sickness and all kinds of disease"* (Matt. 10:1). The authority and power to preach the Kingdom, heal the sick, and cast out unclean spirits are one in the same power. Luke confirms:

> *Then He called His twelve disciples together and gave them power and authority over all demons, and to cure diseases. He sent them to preach the kingdom of God and to heal the sick.... So they departed and went through the towns, preaching the gospel and healing everywhere* (Luke 9:1-2,6).

HEALING AND DELIVERANCE ARE EVIDENCE TO THE UNBELIEVER OF THE POWER AND MERCY OF GOD.

#6: HEALING THE SICK ACCOMPANIES AND AIDS EVANGELISM

Healing and deliverance are evidence to the unbeliever of the power and mercy of God, and they will lead the lost to repentance. Historically, in both Scripture and in the early church, when an evangelist preached, it was the healings that attracted attention and drew people to come and listen. When we today give Jesus proper credit for healing, these supernatural acts stir up belief in Jesus as the Healer, and thus open the way for evangelism—to a profession of faith in God and in Jesus as Lord and Savior. The New Testament is filled with examples of miracles that had an evangelistic impact, some of which we are going to examine in the next chapter.

Chapter 4

EVANGELISM AND HEALING

~~~

In Jesus' ministry, many came to hear His preaching and teaching because He healed the sick. John records:

> *After these things Jesus went over the Sea of Galilee, which is the Sea of Tiberias. Then a great multitude followed Him, because they saw His signs which He performed on those who were diseased* (John 6:1-2).

Jesus clearly stated that His audience should believe in Him because of the signs, wonders, and miracles that accompanied His ministry. These things were not a side item; they were affirmations of His message and identity. Jesus said:

> *If I do not do the works of My Father, do not believe Me: but if I do, though you do not believe Me, believe the works, that you may know and believe that the Father is in Me, and I in Him* (John 10:37-38).

EVANGELISTIC HEALINGS IN
THE ACTS CHURCH

The impact of healings on evangelistic ministry continues in the book of Acts, after Jesus ascended to heaven and then sent the Holy Spirit to empower His people. In Acts 3, we read of the lame man healed by Peter at the gate of the temple called Beautiful. That healing had a powerful evangelistic impact. The lame man's healing drew a crowd and Peter took the opportunity to preach a message of repentance and turning away from sin. *"Now as the lame man who was healed held on to Peter and John, all the people ran together to them in the porch which is called Solomon's, greatly amazed"* (Acts 3:11).

In Acts 9, Peter heals Aeneas at Lydda. Aeneas had been bedridden for eight years and was paralyzed when Jesus healed him. As a result of this miracle, Luke records that *"all who dwelt at Lydda and Sharon saw him and turned to the Lord"* (Acts 9:35).

EVANGELISTIC HEALINGS TODAY

Like the apostle Paul before us, we must recognize the dual nature of the gospel. The gospel is not simply a message of words. It is also a demonstration of power. After having little success preaching to the intellectuals in Athens, Paul went to Corinth where he successfully planted a vital church. The gospel that Paul preached is the same gospel you and I have been called to proclaim today. Here are the words he addressed to the church in Corinth:

And I, brethren, when I came to you, did not come with excellence of speech or of wisdom declaring to you the testimony of God. For I determined not to know anything among you except Jesus Christ and Him crucified. I was with you in weakness, in fear, and in much trembling. And my speech and my preaching were not with persuasive words of human wisdom, but in demonstration of the Spirit and of power, that your faith should not be in the wisdom of men but in the power of God (1 Corinthians 2:1-5).

LIKE THE APOSTLE PAUL BEFORE US, WE MUST
RECOGNIZE THE DUAL NATURE OF THE GOSPEL.
THE GOSPEL IS NOT SIMPLY A MESSAGE OF WORDS.
IT IS ALSO A DEMONSTRATION OF POWER.

Dr. C. Peter Wagner, former professor of church growth at Fuller Theological Seminary, comments on the connection between church growth and healing by divine power in his book *How to Have a Healing Ministry in Any Church.*[1] Wagner says that, on average, by far the greatest church growth in the United States takes place in churches where healing is a regular part of the ministry. He comments further that the greatest church growth in the world is in countries where healing is a regular part of the church's ministry also. He goes on to point out that the amazing, longstanding revival currently going on in China and Argentina is sustained in large measure by churches where healing is a regular part of their ministry.[2]

One must conclude that not only did Jesus see healing as a central part of His ministry when He was on the earth, but He continues to see healing as a central part of what He is doing through the Holy Spirit on the earth today.

GOD HAS COMMISSIONED YOU TO HEAL THE SICK

You have been commissioned to heal the sick. This task is not for a set apart class of highly spiritual people. It was not exclusive to Jesus, the apostles, or even the famous healing evangelists. I wrote a book years ago called *God Can Use Little Ole Me*. I still stand by that message because I was a "little ole me" when the Holy Spirit commissioned me to heal the sick.

SIGNS ARE TO FOLLOW THOSE WHO BELIEVE.

If we are to *fully* preach the whole gospel today, we must model the Lord Jesus and this includes healing the sick. Healing is not intended as an option for us. When Jesus commissioned the disciples to go into the towns and preach the Kingdom of God, that message was tied to a demonstration of healing and delivering power. When we look at the Great Commission in Matthew 28, we see healing and deliverance embraced as a mandate to all believers throughout all the ages. In Mark 16 Jesus clarifies that His commission to us today is no different in demonstration than it was when the disciples walked with Him. Mark's account links the preaching of the gospel to healing the sick and other super-natural phenomena. Just as Jesus instructed the disciples, He is instructing us.

> *Go into all the world and preach the gospel to every creature* [to all creation] *.... And these signs will follow those who believe: In My name they will cast out demons; they will speak with new tongues; they will take up serpents; and if they drink anything deadly, it will by no means hurt them; they will lay hands on the sick, and they will recover* (Mark 16:15,17-18).

Pay attention to the fact that *signs are to follow those who believe.* Are we today not *those who believe?* The words of Scripture include not only those who believed in the days of the first apostles and the early church, but to believers throughout the ages. If the commission to preach the gospel is still in effect for believers today, the sign that we shall lay hands on the sick and the sick will recover is also still in effect.

IF THE COMMISSION TO PREACH THE GOSPEL IS STILL IN EFFECT FOR BELIEVERS TODAY, THE SIGN THAT WE SHALL LAY HANDS ON THE SICK AND THE SICK WILL RECOVER IS ALSO STILL IN EFFECT.

A PRAYER OF IMPARTATION AND BAPTISM IN THE HOLY SPIRIT

Before we end this chapter, I want to pray for you. If you are born again, you have already received the person of the

Holy Spirit who now lives in you. That is part of the miracle of the new birth—God Himself has come to dwell within you. Now that you have received some basic information on *why* we have been called to heal the sick, I want to pray for you to be activated.

It's simple. You don't need to work anything up or try to manufacture an experience. In fact, you may not feel anything at all. Healing the sick is not feeling-based; it's faith-driven. We don't pray for people only when we feel anointed or when we feel some kind of sensation in our hands. Sometimes this happens, but most of the time it does not. We do what Jesus said because He told us to do it, plain and simple. We lay our hands on the sick, in faith, believing that the Spirit of God is the one doing the healing work.

> HEALING THE SICK IS NOT FEELING-BASED; IT'S FAITH-DRIVEN.

I encourage you to stretch out your hands and open them before the Lord, as if you are receiving a gift. Then, simply read these words, receive them in your heart, and believe that you are being activated for supernatural ministry. I recommend you read the prayer slowly, review it several times, and then wait thirty seconds after the "more, Lord" part of the prayer each time. Wait in expectant faith for God's presence to come upon you.

Father, in the name of Jesus, I ask that You would meet the faith and hunger of the person holding this book. I bless this person in the name of Jesus and ask for Your Holy Spirit's fire to come upon them. I ask that You would release Your compassion and love into this person's heart right now. I ask that You would especially impart the gifts of the word of knowledge, healing, prophecy, and the workings of miracles through this person in the days ahead. As they wait in Your presence, Father, with hands outstretched and palms raised, I ask that Your power would touch their hands. Multiply Your power. Increase Your power. Baptize this reader in Your Holy Spirit, and fill their soul with the peace of the Prince of Peace.

More, Lord…

More, Lord…

More, Lord…

In Jesus' name I pray, amen.[3]

NOTES

1. C. Peter Wagner, *How to Have a Healing Ministry in Any Church* (Ventura, CA: Regal Books, 1988).

2. Ibid. See chapter 3 entitled "Power Evangelism Today," starting at page 65; the section "Where God is Moving," 70; description of evangelism in China, 78; and the description of evangelism in Argentina, 81.

3. Randy Clark, *There Is More: The Secret to Experiencing God's Power to Change Your Life* (Grand Rapids: Chosen Books, 2013).

PART 2

INTIMACY

Chapter 5

DISCOVER AND EXPERIENCE

He made known His ways to Moses,
His acts to the children of Israel.
—Psalm 103:7 ESV

THE HEALING WAYS OF GOD

Healing and miracles are the byproducts or fruits of those who enjoy intimate fellowship with God and are committed to doing His works. Once you activate God's power in your life, I want to encourage you to give your life to enjoying intimacy and communion with God. The life of the believer is not simply seeking healings, miracles, signs, and wonders. Those are not the end goals of Christianity. Likewise, Jesus did not paint a picture of the Christian life where these miraculous demonstrations were absent. There is a balance to be maintained.

INVITATION TO FRIENDSHIP AND INTIMACY

Intimacy precedes fruit. To do His works, we first need to know His ways. To move in healing power, we need to first intimately know the Healer. Who are the ones who press in to know the ways of God? They are those whose great prize in life is intimacy with the Father.

TO MOVE IN HEALING POWER, WE NEED TO FIRST INTIMATELY KNOW THE HEALER.

What was Moses' secret to knowing and experiencing the ways of God? Intimacy! While Israel witnessed the miraculous acts of God—which were outstanding and supernatural—Moses *knew* God personally. And one of the very identities that God revealed to Moses was *"I am the Lord who heals you"* (Exod. 15:26). God revealed His identity to Moses in the midst of their intimate relationship.

God reveals His ways to His friends. In Exodus 33:11, we see that *"the Lord would speak to Moses face to face, as one speaks to a friend"* (NIV). Under the Old Testament, friends of God were few and far between. Moses and Abraham are the only two people who are described as *friends* of God under the Old Covenant. This is why Jesus' revelation to His disciples in John 15:14-15 is so incredible. A significant paradigm shift has taken place through the Cross, where a divine communion that was available only to a select, elite few has now been opened to all. Jesus said,

You are My friends if you do whatever I command you. No longer do I call you servants, for a servant does not know what his master is doing; but I have called you friends, for all things that I heard from My Father I have made known to you.

In the Gospel of John, in chapters 14 through 16, Jesus shares His final crucial words with His disciples before His death. There are several key lessons within these passages of Scripture that highlight intimacy with Jesus as it relates to the ministry of healing.

The concepts we are going to examine are simple yet profound. Like many for whom death is imminent, Jesus wanted to share what He felt was most important to those gathered around Him. As I read through these passages, I hear Jesus giving His disciples the secrets of His power and His relationship with the Father that grew out of His obedience.

JESUS TAUGHT THAT ONE OF THE PRIMARY WAYS THAT THE FATHER RECEIVES GLORY IS WHEN THE CHURCH DOES THE WORKS THAT JESUS DID.

THE FATHER RECEIVES GLORY

I want to begin our study of intimacy with John 14:10-14. Within these five verses we find Jesus explaining to the disciples how they can bring glory to God the Father. Jesus is drawing a correlation between works done in His (Jesus') name and the glory the Father receives.

> *Do you not believe that I am in the Father, and the Father in Me? The words that I speak to you I do not speak on My own authority; but the Father who dwells in Me does the works. Believe Me that I am in the Father and the Father in Me, or else believe Me for the sake of the works themselves.*
>
> *Most assuredly, I say to you, he who believes in Me, the works that I do he will do also; and greater works than these he will do, because I go to My Father. And whatever you ask in My name, that I will do, that the Father may be glorified in the Son. If you ask anything in My name, I will do it* (John 14:10-14).

Sometimes Evangelicals get upset with Charismatics and Pentecostals, mistakenly thinking that they are kind of "flakey," just out there looking for some excitement, some "goose bumps." This is not why we pursue the healing ministry. Contrary to popular perception, a good portion of healing ministry is the opposite of goose bumps and spectacle—it is defeat, discouragement, and wondering why some people don't get healed. You will come to greater terms with this in the chapter "The Agony of Defeat."

Nevertheless, Jesus taught that one of the primary ways that the Father receives glory is when the church does the works that Jesus did. If you read John 14-16 in its full context, you will see that Jesus is not just talking about works that we can do in our natural ability. He is talking about works that demand supernatural enablement, supernatural grace. These kinds of works can only be accomplished in the power of the Holy Spirit, and when they are done they bring glory to God.

Jesus wanted His disciples to understand this truth, and He wants the church today to understand it also. In view of this, know that a desire to move in the power and gifts of the Holy Spirit it is not a flaky charismatic notion. Moving in the power gifts of the Spirit is just as honorable and noble as walking in the fruit of the Spirit, and is essential if we are to bring glory to God. Jesus was always motivated by a desire to bring glory to God and we should be also.

WALKING IN THE FRUIT OF THE SPIRIT IS ESSENTIAL IF WE ARE TO BRING GLORY TO GOD.

ANOINTED FOR WORKS... AND GREATER WORKS

Many people, when they read John 14:12, wonder who Jesus is speaking to in this passage. He says, *"Most assuredly, I say to you, he who believes in Me, the works that I do he will do also; and greater works than these he will do, because I go to My Father."* Some claim that He was only speaking to the apostles, but when we closely examine this verse we see that is not the case. The only condition here is belief. He does not say, "I tell you the truth, the apostles who have faith in Me will do what I have been doing..." Rather, He says that "anyone who believers in Me..." Many have tried to take the words of Jesus here and say that they apply only to the elders of the church, but that is not what Jesus said.

I have a friend who is an elder in a church near my home. He is a chiropractor. One of his employees is a Christian. We were talking one day and I asked this employee if she prayed for the people they treated. Her response was, "Oh, no. I would never pray for anybody." I said, "Well, why not?" and she said, "Well, in James 5 it says to let the elders pray for the sick—to call for the elders. We believe in healing and we let the elders of our church pray for the sick, but only the elders." This is a common view held by many in the church, but it is not what Jesus said in John 14:12. He was speaking to all of us—anyone who believes in Him.

JESUS' PRIMARY ASSIGNMENT WAS NOT TO COME AND BE GOD ON THE EARTH; IT WAS TO BECOME FULLY HUMAN WHILE ALSO BEING FULLY GOD.

And if we study this passage a little more closely, we see that Jesus has attached a condition to His promise. He tells us that we must have *faith* in Him if we are to do the works that He did. Faith is the condition needed for this promise to become reality. We must be careful not to emphasize the promises of Jesus and skip the conditions—that is not biblical.

There are people who will ask, "If we are to do what Jesus did and more, why are we not seeing the 'more' spoken of here?" They say that the ministry of Jesus was a short three years, but we have much more time, so why are we not seeing more miracles? Their reasoning is that more of the miraculous would detract from Jesus, but I completely disagree. I think more miracles would actually bolster His ministry. Jesus' primary assignment was not to come and be God on the earth; it was to become fully human while also being fully God.

I believe that Jesus Christ was very God of very God and very man of very man without being a *tertium quid*, as the Creed of Chalcedon said. A *tertium quid* means a third type of being. When we see Jesus we see God, because Jesus Himself tells us, *"He who has seen Me has seen the Father"* (John 14:9), and *"I and My Father are one"* (John 10:30). Jesus was perfectly yielded to the Father's will. He never violated the Father's intentions. Everything that Jesus did was a perfect reflection of who the Father is. Paul writes in Colossians 1:15 that *"Christ is the visible image of the invisible God"* (NLT).

EVERYTHING THAT JESUS DID WAS A PERFECT
REFLECTION OF WHO THE FATHER IS.

When we fully understand this concept, it becomes evident that Jesus died not just so we could go to heaven. Jesus wanted to do more than just get us to heaven. He wanted to create a community of believers who could bring heaven to earth by the power that was going to be given in His name. The Bible teaches much more than salvation in the afterlife. When Jesus defines eternal life, He does not just describe a post-death experience where we live forever in heaven. He said, *"Now this is eternal life: that they know You, the only true God, and Jesus Christ, whom You have sent"* (John 17:3 NIV).

Chapter 6

RECEIVE THE SPIRIT OF CHRIST

A CHARISMATIC COMMUNITY

Jesus died so that the people of God could receive the Holy Spirit and become a charismatic community living in intimacy with Him. When I say *charismatic*, I am talking about those who are endowed with grace. The word *charismatic* comes from the Greek term, *charismata*, in 1 Corinthians 12, which means gracelets, grace gifts, and the gift of the Holy Spirit. We are talking about God Himself coming upon us, about being rooted in grace. The Holy Spirit no longer just comes upon prophets, priests, and kings as He did in the Old Testament. Under the New Covenant, the Holy Spirit now comes upon all of God's people. (See Acts 2:17 and Joel 2:28.) We are able to experience conversion and regeneration in a way that the people of the Old Testament were not. We have God in us *and* upon us, and when He comes upon us, He writes His law in our hearts and then gives us the power to live out His will.

***

JESUS DIED SO THAT THE PEOPLE OF GOD COULD RECEIVE THE HOLY SPIRIT AND BECOME A CHARISMATIC COMMUNITY LIVING IN INTIMACY WITH HIM.

***

You might still be saying that you cannot believe that the words of Jesus actually mean "greater things," but I know a man who has raised four people from the dead. We only have reference to Jesus raising three from the dead. In fact, this man has raised four people from the dead, and his brother, who is illiterate, has raised seven! Many people who hear such testimonies gawk in disbelief. Whether they believe it or not, it is true. These miraculous demonstrations of raising the dead and healing bring great glory to God.

Jesus died so that men like these, and many others, could, in fact, raise the dead. Jesus died so that even illiterate men could have power in His name, because it was not my friend or his brother who raised the dead, it was the power of the Holy Spirit that was on Jesus who came upon these two men and raised eleven people from the dead. These men were simply the vessels through which the Holy Spirit was working, and that same Holy Spirit is now able to come upon all people today. Paul confirmed this when he wrote, *"The Spirit of Him who raised Jesus from the dead dwells in you"* (Rom. 8:11).

This new relationship where God lives inside of us was made possible because Jesus went to the cross. Yes, Jesus died for our salvation, and I forever thank God for that. And heaven is fully coming to earth in the second coming, when Jesus returns. Until that time, however, God desires to fashion a people on the earth who, by the power of His Spirit, will be able to live and have a relationship with Him in order that He may establish His Kingdom on the earth. Out of this relationship, we live empowered by the Spirit to deliver people from damnation, death, disease, and those troubled by demons.

GOD DESIRES TO FASHION A PEOPLE ON THE EARTH WHO, BY THE POWER OF HIS SPIRIT, WILL BE ABLE TO LIVE AND HAVE A RELATIONSHIP WITH HIM IN ORDER THAT HE MAY ESTABLISH HIS KINGDOM ON THE EARTH.

The apostle Paul said that the god of this world (Satan) blinds those who do not accept the gospel (see 2 Cor. 4:4). When Adam and Eve rebelled in the garden of Eden, they handed over their authority to Satan. Jesus came that we might gain that authority back; that we might have the power to defeat the enemy and to live as the people of God, manifesting His mercy and power. Jesus' death made this all possible.

As a result of embracing this perspective of the gospel, we are authorized to do what Jesus did and even greater things. When He tells His disciples in John 16:10, *"I am going to the Father,"* He is telling them that He is getting ready to be crucified, and then lifted up in the resurrection, which will be followed by being lifted up in ascension. Then, in John 16:13, He explains, *"When He, the Spirit of truth, has come, He will guide you into all truth; for He will not speak on His own authority, but whatever He hears He will speak; and He will tell you things to come."* In the next verse Jesus tells us the purpose for all of this: *"He will glorify Me, for He will take of what is Mine and declare it to you"* (John 16:14). This is a picture of the Trinity. We ask the Father in the name of Jesus, the Holy Spirit comes and enables us because Jesus has given us the authority, and this in turn brings glory to the Father and the Son.

THIS IS A PICTURE OF THE TRINITY. WE ASK THE FATHER IN THE NAME OF JESUS, THE HOLY SPIRIT COMES AND ENABLES US BECAUSE JESUS HAS GIVEN US THE AUTHORITY, AND THIS IN TURN BRINGS GLORY TO THE FATHER AND THE SON.

A PROMISE OF POWER

Look back at John 14:14 for a moment. This Scripture contains a powerful promise. Jesus tells us, *"If you ask anything in My name, I will do it."* He is saying that when our will is in line with His will, whatever we ask in His name, He will do it for us.

The Hebraic understanding of a name is that it represents the character and nature of the person it belongs to.

Therefore, when Jesus instructs us to "ask in His name," it means that whatever we ask must be in line with His character, His nature. This is the basis of our authority—not a magic wand or formula to get whatever we want from God. We cannot ask for something in the name of Jesus that is contrary to His nature and expect His cooperation. Yet, when we ask in line with His will, the possibilities truly are endless. In the later part of John 14:14, Jesus says, *"I will do it."* What a promise! What authority has been given to us!

INTIMACY'S RELATIONSHIP TO REVELATION, MANIFESTATION, VISITATION, AND HABITATION

Our intimacy with God has a unique relationship to four things: revelation, manifestation, visitation, and habitation. Again, Jesus tells His disciples,

> *If you love Me, keep My commandments. And I will pray to the Father, and He will give you another Helper, that He may abide with you forever—the Spirit of truth, whom the world cannot receive, because it neither sees Him nor knows Him; but you know Him, for He dwells with you and will be in you. I will not leave you orphans; I will come to you. A little while longer and the world will see Me no more, but you will see Me. Because I live, you will live also. At that day you will know that I am in My Father, and you in Me, and I in you* (John 14:15-20).

Revelation

Pay careful attention to what Jesus is saying here: "To the person who loves Me (Jesus), I will *reveal* Myself. To the person who obeys Me, I will *reveal* Myself." Jesus is making a strong connection between revelation (hearing from the Father) and sanctification (obedience). He is telling us to obey Him because we love Him. Then He goes on to say:

> *"He who has My commandments and keeps them, it is he who loves Me. And he who loves Me will be loved by My Father, and I will love him and manifest Myself to him."*
>
> *Judas* (not Iscariot) *said to Him, "Lord, how is it that You will manifest Yourself to us, and not to the world?" Jesus answered and said to him, "If anyone loves Me, he will keep My word; and My Father will love him, and We will come to him and make Our home with him"* (John 14:21-23).

"We will come to him and make Our home with him." How is this even possible? What Jesus is saying is that when the Holy Spirit comes in you, the Father and the Son are in you as well because of the nature of the Trinity. There is a relationship between intimacy with Jesus and the manifestation (or revelation) of Jesus, and visitation (or habitation) of the Father and the Son with us. The "habitation" we are speaking of here is Jesus in us. The habitation of Jesus in us is the reality we are called to live in and live from. However, sometimes we grieve the One in us to such an extent that some of His revelation gets blocked.

Obedience

If we desire this kind of intimacy with the Trinity, we must first understand its connection to obedience. In John 14:15, Jesus says, *"If you love Me, you will obey what I command."* We are not saved by obedience, but we can enjoy intimacy with Jesus if we obey Him. If we start violating this request for obedience by saying yes to the things we want to do and no to things we don't want to do, without regard to His will, it will affect our intimacy and our revelation.

WE ARE NOT SAVED BY OBEDIENCE, BUT WE CAN ENJOY INTIMACY WITH JESUS IF WE OBEY HIM.

In John 14:16-17, Jesus shows us the connection between obedience and receiving the Holy Spirit: *"And I will pray the Father, and He will give you another Helper, that He may abide with you forever—the Spirit of truth."* Understand that this obedience is not possible apart from the renewing and regenerating work of the Holy Spirit within us. Then in verses 21 and 23 we see obedience linked to intimacy and intimacy to the revelation of Jesus—when God speaks to you. (I am talking about revelation in the sense of when God speaks to us.) In John 10:27, Jesus says, *"My sheep hear My voice, and I know them, and they follow Me."*

God still speaks! There really is communication between God and His people today. We do not need to complicate it. When He tells us something or reveals something to us, we simply need to learn to accept it and be obedient to it. Others may try and complicate the issue, but I encourage you to keep it simple. Do not worry, trying to discern, "Was that a prophetic word, or a word of knowledge, or a word of wisdom?" The package is not as important as what is inside. Do not get distracted by the form of the message—simply receive God's voice as He speaks.

WE SHOW THE WORLD THAT WE ARE DISCIPLES OF JESUS, NOT ONLY BY THE WAY WE LOVE ONE ANOTHER, BUT ALSO WHEN WE BEAR FRUIT FOR THE KINGDOM.

INTIMACY'S RELATIONSHIP TO FRUITFULNESS, POWER, AND HEALING

Now that we have laid a foundation, I want you to see clearly the relationship between intimacy, fruitfulness, and healing. Jesus tells us,

> *Abide in Me, and I in you. As the branch cannot bear fruit of itself, unless it abides in the vine, neither can you, unless you abide in Me. I am the vine, you are the branches. He who abides in Me, and I in him, bears much fruit; for without Me you can do nothing* (John 15:4-5).

We show the world that we are disciples of Jesus, not only by the way we love one another, but also when we bear fruit for the Kingdom. This is *not* the fruit that we commonly call the *fruit of the Spirit* that is listed in Galatians

5:22-23: *"love, joy, peace, longsuffering, kindness, goodness, faithfulness, gentleness, self-control."*

Of course, we should have these fruits or evidences of the Spirit in our lives. However, in John 15 the *fruits* Jesus is referring to are not things we can accomplish through discipline alone. In the context of this passage, Jesus is talking about fruits as being the *works* that He says we will do. The context indicates this is a different use of fruit than Paul used in Galatians 5. Instead of the fruit of *being*, Jesus is speaking in the gospel of John about the fruit of *doing*. The fruits of the Spirit are the character traits of Jesus being made manifest in our lives. They change the way we are. The fruit of John 15 describes what we are empowered to *do* because we are in fellowship and intimacy with God.

In these verses, Jesus is saying that it is to the Father's glory that we as Christians bear much fruit from the works that can only be accomplished through the power of His Spirit. This includes, among other things, healing the sick! If we could do these exploits in our flesh, they would not bring glory to God. It is the *"Me in you—the Father and I in you"* intimate exchange that enables us to accomplish what we are being commissioned to do, and even greater things! By bearing this fruit, God receives much glory.

There is a commensurate relationship between how much glory is given to God and how much the church, out of obedience and intimacy, receives revelation from God of what He wants us to do in and through us. The stronger this relationship, the more we can act in faith and the authority of His name. This is when we begin to see miracles, signs, and wonders take place. We cannot *do* what we have not first seen. In other words, if we don't have a clear vision that God desires to heal the sick—and don't understand that healing gives God glory—we won't step out and operate in the ministry of healing.

WE HAVE A LIMITED PERSPECTIVE OF WHAT CAN AND DOES GIVE GOD THE GLORY HE DESERVES.

As Christians, we all desire to give God glory. That is a given. I am afraid, though, that this language of "glory" has become too commonplace among us. We say it, but I think we have a limited perspective of what can and does give God the glory He deserves. Let's not be narrow-minded when we think of God's glory.

This is not a call to replace the fruit of the Spirit from Galatians 5 with the fruit of John 15. Likewise, we should not replace the fruit of John 15 with the fruit of Galatians 5. We need both in our lives since it is through both kinds of fruit that God will be fully glorified. Specifically, in the context of the healing ministry, it is the fruit of John 15 that will bring God glory.

When you remain in God—as you draw close to Him, discovering His character and nature—you learn what gives Him glory. I encourage you to go back to John 14-17. Though these Scriptures do not overtly talk about healing ministry, their principles are absolutely fundamental to our understanding of Jesus' commission to us. Soak in these passages of Scripture because they are inviting you into a life of supernatural fruitfulness. Do not think you need to pursue one expression of fruit above the other. It is not Christian character *or* supernatural power. Jesus invited you into both. The closer you get to Jesus, the more you should desire to reflect Him in every way possible—in both His nature and demonstration.

THE CLOSER YOU GET TO JESUS, THE
MORE YOU SHOULD DESIRE TO REFLECT
HIM IN EVERY WAY POSSIBLE—IN BOTH
HIS NATURE AND DEMONSTRATION.

Remember this: Jesus did not intend for the Father to be glorified for just the first 300 years of history after His crucifixion, until the church was formally established. Jesus desires for the Father to be glorified on the earth until the second coming. If the way in which we glorify God is to perform these works—works that cannot be done in the flesh—then the "gifts" and endowments of supernatural power must continue. They are the divine enablements of the Holy Spirit in our lives. Without them, we are reduced simply to what we can accomplish in the flesh.

Chapter 7

ABIDING

THE PRIORITY OF GOD'S WORD

If anyone does not abide in Me, he is cast out as a branch and is withered; and they gather them and throw them into the fire, and they are burned. If you abide in Me, and My words abide in you, you will ask what you desire, and it shall be done for you. By this My Father is glorified, that you bear much fruit; so you will be My disciples (John 15:6-8).

Intimacy and supernatural fruitfulness are both dependent upon abiding in Christ, which means specifically, keeping His Word. In verse 7, Jesus begins with the word *if:* "*If you abide in Me, and My words abide in you, you will ask what you desire, and it shall be done for you.*"

His Word must be our priority because it informs us of what we can legally ask God for. The Word keeps us on track to make requests and declare commands that are in line with God's nature. It is so important that we know what the Word says in order to ask in line with God's nature and will. Jesus is clearly not saying, "You can have an experience with God and never study the Bible." Think about it. If we do not know the Word of God and do not know our identity in Christ, then we are not going to be as fit for the Master's use as we could be if we knew His words. *"If you abide in Me, and My words abide in you, you will ask what you desire, and it shall be done for you"* (John 15:7).

WHEN YOU RECEIVE A RHEMA WORD, IT CARRIES INHERENT POWER TO TURN THE WORD RECEIVED INTO REALITY RELEASED.

We have a tendency to read this passage as if it *only* refers to the Bible, when in fact it refers to both the written Scriptures *and* also to any freshly spoken *rhema* word of God. Immediately, some will take issue with equating this kind of *freshly spoken* word of God to Scripture. This is not a call to uphold prophetic utterances to the same level as Scripture. In order to evaluate whether we have received a legitimate *rhema* word of God, we need to be intimate with God, the author of the Word. When we start to intimately know God's character, it becomes easier for us to evaluate whether or not something is of God.

When you receive a *rhema* word, it carries inherent power to turn the word received into reality released. A *rhema* word can be given through an individual or come directly from God Himself, and it will focus on something specific you are to do. The ability to perform the word is locked in the word itself. This is why the faith factor is so important. Paul said in 2 Corinthians 4:13, *"I believed and therefore I spoke."* Revelation causes faith, and faith gives us a foundation for confession. First, Paul received (revelation); second, Paul believed (faith); and third, Paul confessed (he spoke).

If we have His word abiding in us—the word that comes to us from the Spirit—it will create great faith to speak out God's word and supernatural things will be wrought in Jesus' name.

WHEN WE KNOW THE WAYS OF GOD
WE ARE POSITIONED TO BETTER LEARN
HOW TO CO-LABOR WITH HIM.

KNOW HIS WAYS, BEAR MUCH FRUIT, GIVE GOD GLORY

When we know the ways of God we are positioned to better learn how to co-labor with Him. Revelation is what exposes us to the Spirit's movement in the world. We have the chance to participate or disengage. Since we live here on planet earth, this is the only place we have the opportunity to give God glory. Moses asked of the Lord, *"Show me Your ways"* (Exod. 33:13). Jesus said, *"By this My Father is glorified, that you bear much fruit; so you will be My disciples"* (John 15:8).

When we bear fruit, we reveal that we are truly Jesus' disciples. This is simple, but what does it say about church life when this is not happening? When the Christian life is reduced to upholding good morals and religious duty, this type of "life" does not bring the full amount of glory to the Father. Our quest and desire for spiritual gifts and supernatural power is so that our lives will bring God the full measure of glory that He deserves, not so we can have a "good feeling." We don't ask God to bless what we're doing; instead, we intentionally bless what He is doing.

Some people label healing as a secondary, if not inferior, ministry, because it addresses the physical and not the spiritual. But this is nothing more than modern Gnostic thought in action—an early church heresy that continues to rear its head today. Body, soul, and spirit—all three realms of life can, and, in fact, do, give God glory. Healing of the body is but one example, but an important one. If Jesus did only what He saw His Father doing, and since He was so actively engaged in healing ministry during His time on earth, then healing was and is not a peripheral issue to God.

WE DON'T ASK GOD TO BLESS WHAT WE'RE DOING; INSTEAD, WE INTENTIONALLY BLESS WHAT HE IS DOING.

When I was pastoring a church, my desire was that we would be a church that brought glory to the Father, not just on Sundays through worship, but every day in every way—by hearing what He said to us, stepping out with what we heard, and believing that He wanted to use us as salt and light throughout our daily lives.

THE GREAT COMMISSION

Go therefore and make disciples of all the nations, baptizing them in the name of the Father and of the Son and of the Holy Spirit, teaching them to observe all things that I have commanded you; and lo, I am with you always, even to the end of the age. (Matthew 28:19)

JESUS' COMMISSIONING IS FOR POWER AS MUCH AS IT IS FOR CHARACTER.

The church has often appropriated this commission from Jesus as if it proposed another moral command—as if the Great Commission was the New Testament continuation of the Ten Commandments. While we certainly ought to obey the Ten Commandments and the other moral commandments found in Scripture, we are missing something when we reduce this commission to just moral instruction. What are the *"all things that I have commanded you"* Jesus is talking about here? Character is obviously a key part of it, based on what we see in the Sermon on the Mount. However, Jesus' commissioning is for power as much as it is for character.

The same is true for a passage like Ephesians 2:10, where Paul writes that *"we are His workmanship, created in Christ*

Jesus for good works, which God prepared beforehand that we should walk in them." When Paul describes the good works that we were predestined to walk in, he is talking about more than charity, good deeds, and upstanding moral character. To understand this truth, we must move past the wrong teaching that has pervaded the church for hundreds of years.

If we believe that God has stopped doing the miraculous, we will literally read the supernatural right out of the Bible. It would follow then, that the good works in Ephesians 2:10 could not possibly mean healings, signs, and wonders, since God no longer does those things. The same would be true for Matthew 28 in the Great Commission. If we buy into a system that has rejected the miraculous, Jesus' commission would look much different. It is wrong teaching like this that has caused us to relegate the good works that we do see to mere moral deeds, divorcing them from the demonstrations of power that Jesus did throughout His ministry. In truth, these are the good works God prepared in advance for us to do.

HEALING ACTUALLY REPRESENTS THE VERY
NATURE AND CHARACTER OF GOD IN THE EARTH.

We must approach the ministry of healing from the foundation that we have divine authority in Christ. As we draw close to Him in the place of intimacy, we discover who He is and what He is like through revelation. Healing is no longer some peripheral ministry, nor do we view it as part of some "name it and claim it" Christian subculture. Healing actually represents the very nature and character of God in the earth. This is what you and I get to participate in as we pray for the sick—we will see the Spirit's power released, and give the Father the glory He deserves. This is your mission and this is my mission, now, today!

PART 3

PRAYER

Chapter 8

A PLACE TO START

You may be asking yourself, "How do I start ministering to the sick?" It is simple. You must first step out in faith. *Getting started* is the first step. The next few chapters will give you inspirational stories to build your faith, keys to persevere through discouragement, and practical ways to help determine the level of faith of those you are ministering to.

GOD WILL NOT FIT INTO A MODEL

I want to give you a practical, user-friendly resource to help you start ministering to the sick, however, I have to warn and encourage you from the start about using any kind of model. First, the warning: God will not fit in any box, even those created by our well-intentioned models, principles, and standard methods of operation. At the day's end, healing ministry is not about using a certain kind of model; it's about people encountering the Healer. It's not about principles; it's about presence.

As you will discover, God is notorious for working outside of the boundaries we tend to establish through our principles—yes, even principles we have based on our study of Scripture. When God moves outside of these perimeters, He is not violating His Word; He never violates His Word. However, He will often operate in unique, different ways that prevent us from definitively concluding, "This is how God will heal...if you follow this process, you will experience guaranteed results." I've been guilty of this before. I remember years ago being challenged by a Christian leader for putting God "in a box" because I was stringently adhering to certain formulas and systems. If God did not operate in agreement with a certain principle, then I assumed that He could not work. This is such a limited view of Almighty God, and I am so grateful that He has upgraded my perspective.

GOD IS NOTORIOUS FOR WORKING
OUTSIDE OF THE BOUNDARIES WE TEND TO
ESTABLISH THROUGH OUR PRINCIPLES.

So again, be warned: God will not fit in any box you construct for Him. In fact, if we think we have got God's ways and methods figured out, chances are we are further away from knowing Him than we originally thought. If our *god* fits in a box, it's *not* the God of Scripture; it's a god we've constructed in our own image. That is the warning.

Here is the encouragement. I work with a five-step prayer model, which I am going to outline for you. This model gives you a very practical starting point when you are ministering healing. Just don't get discouraged when God works or moves outside of this model. It's only meant to be a helpful tool, not a confining prison.

IF WE THINK WE HAVE GOT GOD'S WAYS AND METHODS FIGURED OUT, CHANCES ARE WE ARE FURTHER AWAY FROM KNOWING HIM THAN WE ORIGINALLY THOUGHT.

Models like this are important for those who are beginning to step out and heal the sick. They give you something practical to work with as you move into unfamiliar territory. Before I give you a full breakdown of the five-step prayer model though, I want to give you some tips to help prepare you to walk in God's healing power. These are applicable whether you are ministering healing by yourself in the course of your everyday life, or you are leading a ministry/church group that does outreach to the sick.

BE PREPARED

Preparation for healing ministry is very important. I encourage you to live in a state of expectation and preparation because you never know when God might lead you to pray for someone—a family member, a friend, a coworker, or a person you come across throughout your day. The following are practical steps that will assist you in becoming better prepared for ministry:

1. Try to be a clean, clear vessel for God to use.

2. Be "prayed up!" Pray in the Holy Spirit (in tongues) because this will increase your sensitivity to God's leading and direction when it comes to praying for people. If you don't pray in tongues, ask God fervently and specifically to be with you and to help you. He is the Healer. If He doesn't come and release His power, the person you pray for won't get healed. Remember, you do not have the power to heal; only God does.

3. Take a moment to ask the Holy Spirit if there is anyone you need to forgive. If there is, forgive him or her at once, from your heart (see Matt. 6:14-15).

4. Ask the Holy Spirit to show you any unconfessed sin in your life; if He does, sincerely repent at once and ask God's forgiveness. (see Luke 13:2-5).

5. Ask God to give you His love for each person you pray for. This is another way we follow the model of Jesus—responding to the sicknesses and infirmities of people with God's compassion. A loving ministry will impact the sick person for good, whether or not their infirmity is healed. Either way, your ministry may be a person's first experience with God's love.

Now you are ready to examine the five-step prayer model!

Chapter 9

THE FIVE-STEP PRAYER MODEL

As I explained before, there are many different ways of praying for the sick. Following this five-step model is not the only way. If you have found one that is effective for you, I encourage you to use it in your own personal ministry. If you are just starting out praying for healing, however, this five-step model is a simple, easy, and clear method that will get you going. We use this model in our ministry, Global Awakening, and see its impact around the world. We train our ministry teams using this particular model because it is quiet, loving, and effective and can be used by anyone. This is how we get the "little ole mes" confidently releasing God's power in dramatic, supernatural ways.[1]

FIVE STEPS

1. Interview

2. Diagnosis and Prayer Selection

3. Prayer Ministry

4. Re-interview

5. Post Prayer Suggestions

STEP ONE: THE INTERVIEW

Briefly interview the person who is requesting healing prayer. Be attentive and gentle. A loving attitude on your part will do much to reassure the person that he or she is in good hands. Remember, whether the people you pray for are healed or not, it is most important that they leave feeling loved because of their interaction with you.

Start by asking the person about their physical need, but do not let the conversation go into lengthy detail. For example, you can begin like this:

"What is your name?" (A question or two to put the person at ease.)

"What would you like prayer for?"

"How long have you had this condition?"

"Do you know what the cause is?"

"Have you seen a doctor?" "What does he or she say is the matter?"

"Do you remember what was happening in your life when this condition began?"

"Did anything traumatic happen to you about the time your condition began, or within a few months prior to it starting?"

You may need to explain to the person being prayed for why you are asking these last two questions because their answers play an important role in *how* you end up praying for them.

These questions are often sufficient for the initial interview. You may now know the nature and cause of the condition. In some cases, you will not know and might need to ask additional questions or invite the Holy Spirit to provide additional details. If His leading is not clear to you, you may need to make an educated guess as to the nature or cause of the condition.

The interview stage is absolutely necessary if you are going to pray for the person correctly. If you are unable to determine a possible cause for the person's injury or issue remember, God is gracious and merciful. He is faithful to operate beyond the parameters of our formulas and principles.

STEP TWO: PRAYER SELECTION

After interviewing the person you should hopefully have enough information to select the appropriate kind of prayer to meet the person's unique needs. The two most common kinds of prayer to use when praying for the sick are the petition prayer and the command prayer. We must work with the Holy Spirit and specifically ask for His discernment as to which one to use.

The Petition Prayer is a request to heal, addressed to God, to Jesus, or to the Holy Spirit. Here are some examples.

"Father, in the name of Jesus, I ask You to restore sight to this eye."

"Father, I pray in Jesus' name, come and straighten this spine."

"Father, release Your power to heal, in Jim's body, in the name of Jesus."

"Come, Holy Spirit. Release Your power. Touch Jim's back, in Jesus' name."

The Command Prayer is just that—a command addressed to a condition of the body, or to a part of the body, or to a troubling spirit, such as a spirit of pain, or infirmity, or of affliction.

"In the name of Jesus, I command this tumor to shrivel up and dissolve."

"In the name of Jesus, spine, be straight! Be healed!"

"In Jesus' name, I command every afflicting spirit: get out of Jim's body."

"In the name of Jesus, I command all pain and swelling to leave this ankle."

Here are examples of situations where a command prayer is appropriate:

- As your initial step, unless you are led otherwise by the Holy Spirit.

- When there has been a word of knowledge for healing or some other indication that God wants to heal the person at this time.

- When petition prayers have been tried and progress has stopped.

- When casting out an afflicting spirit or any other spirit.

- When a curse or vow is broken.

- Whenever you are so led by the Holy Spirit to make such a command.

Once you have selected the appropriate type of prayer, you are ready to begin the third step—prayer ministry.

WE MUST REMAIN MINDFUL THAT IT IS THE SPIRIT OF GOD ALONE WHO POSSESSES AND RELEASES HEALING POWER.

STEP THREE: PRAYER MINISTRY

The person of the Holy Spirit is not an add-on when it comes to praying for the sick. He is the One who releases God's healing power *through you* to the afflicted individual. I encourage you to begin praying by audibly asking the Holy Spirit to come. You can simply say, "Come, Holy Spirit!" or, "Come, Holy Spirit, with Your healing power." Or you may prefer a longer prayer. Once you have invited the Holy Spirit to come, wait on Him for a minute or two. When people get caught up in healing formulas or principles, it becomes easy to neglect the most fundamental and vital component—God

Himself. We must remain mindful that it is the Spirit of God alone who possesses and releases healing power.

Next, tell the person who is receiving ministry that you are going to be silent for a minute or two so that they do not become confused while you are quietly listening to the Holy Spirit.

AN ATTITUDE OF RECEIVING

Encourage the person not to pray while you are praying for him or her. Here again, be gentle and loving. Say something like: "When you are praying in English, or in tongues or thanking Jesus, or saying '*Yes, Yes!*' it is harder for me to focus on your body and to pay attention to what the Holy Spirit is doing. It is also harder for you to receive healing. I know this means a lot to you, and you have probably prayed a lot about your condition, but for right now, I need you to focus on your body. I want you to relax and to let me know if anything begins to happen in your body—like heat, tingling, electricity, or a change in the amount or location of the pain."

JESUS DID NOT COMMISSION US SIMPLY TO PRAY FOR THE SICK; WE ARE TO HEAL THE SICK THROUGH HIS POWER.

Sometimes the person may find it very difficult *not* to pray while you are ministering to them. Do not get hung up on this. Persevere and pray for the person anyway. If the presence of the Holy Spirit becomes evident—the person is feeling heat or tingling or some other manifestation or sensation—continue waiting on the Holy Spirit until He finishes what He wishes to do at that time. When the manifestation has ebbed, check to see if the healing is complete.

PRAY IN JESUS' NAME WITH EXPECTATION AND CONFIDENCE

If the healing is not complete, continue to minister. Remember, always pray or command *in the name of Jesus!* Jesus did not commission us simply to pray for the sick; we are to *heal* the sick through His power. Jesus said, *"In My name…they will lay hands on the sick, and they will recover"* (Mark 16:17-18). We must approach healing ministry with this expectation, always mindful that it is not up to us to do the healing; it is the Holy Spirit's function.

We can never use the name of Jesus too much when ministering healing. Healing power is released through His name alone. Some who have anointed healing ministries will often simply repeat "in the name of Jesus," over and over as their prayer for healing.

THANK GOD FOR WHAT HE IS DOING

It is very important to thank God while He is healing the person instead of waiting until the healing is complete. We can never thank God too much. Thanksgiving offers God the glory that is due His name, and lifts our faith. Thanksgiving will shift our perspective. Instead of focusing on the 50 percent that is not yet healed, thank God for bringing supernatural improvement to the 50 percent that He has just touched with His power. Your faith will increase and so will the person's you are praying for.

DEAL WITH THE CAUSE AND SYMPTOMS

When you minister healing, speak to the cause of the condition, if you know the cause, as well as to the symptoms. For example:

> "Father, in Jesus' name, I ask You to heal the cones and rods in the retina of this eye. Father, in the name of Jesus, cause the scar tissue to dissolve and leave this eye. Oh God, restore the sight in this eye, in the name of Jesus."

> "In the name of Jesus, I command this ruptured disc to be healed and filled with fluid, and every pinched nerve to be released and soothed. I command the pain to leave Joe's back."

> "In the name of Jesus, dear God, I ask You to heal this pancreas. Father, in the name of Jesus, I ask You to touch this pancreas with Your healing power and cause it to function normally. Cause it to produce insulin as needed and cause all diabetes to be cured and complete health restored. Release Your healing in the name of Jesus."

> "In the name of Jesus, I command every afflicting spirit and every spirit of infirmity to leave Jane's body now!"

"In Jesus' name, I command all stiffness to leave this joint, all pain to leave, and all swelling to subside. I command all calcium deposits and all scar tissue to dissolve in Jesus' name."

"In Jesus' name, I command all chemical imbalances in Joe's body to be healed."

"I command every organ furnishing chemicals or other signals to his organs to function normally in Jesus' name."

THE POWER AND FREEDOM OF FORGIVENESS

Forgiveness is essential if healing is to talk place, and can be an obstacle to healing if left unresolved. If it appears that someone else caused the condition or that someone wronged the person around the time the condition started, find out if the sick person has forgiven the offending person. If not, forgiveness should precede your prayer for healing. Sometimes, we need to forgive ourselves, or even God.

Here is an example of a situation necessitating forgiveness. A woman has had arthritis in her spine for five years, ever since her husband ran off with another woman. It's important to identify whether or not she has forgiven her husband and the other woman involved in the affair. Jesus did not suggest forgiveness as optional or just highly recommended (see Matt. 6:14-15; Mark 11:25). He said that forgiveness it is something we *must* do.

I once prayed for a pastor who had suffered with back pain for ten years. Ten years prior a split occurred in his church and some of his closet friends were involved. Several had turned against him. When he was able to forgive the ringleaders and everyone else involved, he was healed. His forgiveness unlocked his healing. I didn't even have to pray for his healing. It is not uncommon for a person to be healed before you begin praying for them if they forgive those who hurt them, and repent and ask God's forgiveness for the sins of resentment and anger.

REPENTANCE

If it appears to you the condition was brought on by sin, very gently inquire of the person if this might be the case. If this leading is from the Holy Spirit, the Spirit will usually indicate the specific sin that is the problem. There are many different ways you can determine if the sickness was brought about by sin. The Holy Spirit might reveal something to you through a word of knowledge, or perhaps the initial interview suggests that sin played a role in bringing on the sickness. However the information comes, it is important for you to handle the issue of sin delicately.

As you address the root causes of sin, always proceed with tenderness and sensitivity. Never accuse the person confrontationally of causing the condition by their sin. General accusations of sin are often destructive and probably are from the enemy. You are not an agent of God's wrath and judgment; you are simply an ambassador and representative of His love. The only reason God would have you work through matters of sin with a person is to address specific barriers that might be blocking the flow of His healing power. Ask if perhaps the condition could be related to a particular kind of lifestyle or choice. You might say something like, "I wonder if this condition could be related to things you have done in the past."

If the person you are praying for agrees that sin might have opened the door to sickness, encourage them to repent and ask for God's forgiveness. Their repentance and forgiveness should precede your prayer for healing. Sin that is not repented of can impede healing. Anger can contribute to back pain and some forms of depression. AIDS may be the result of an immoral lifestyle. Smoking might have brought on lung cancer. These are not curses or judgments sent directly from God, but rather they are the results of sinful choices and actions.

KEYS FOR MINISTERING TO THE SICK

Listen to the Holy Spirit

Although I have already mentioned many times how important it is to listen to the Holy Spirit during prayer ministry, I am including it here again, in first place on the list of keys for ministering to the sick. We must be tuned into the voice of the Holy Spirit on a moment-by-moment basis while participating in any kind of healing ministry, because He may give us guidance that we would otherwise miss. He is our source of all power and wisdom. We can clearly see this modeled in the life of Jesus as He healed people in many different ways.

Short Prayers

If you notice changes in the person's condition, it is appropriate and often helpful to pray short prayers or give brief commands. Short prayers enable you to immediately evaluate what is working and what isn't. If partial healing follows a long prayer, it is hard to know what part of the lengthy prayer or command was effective. Thus, the entire prayer may have to be repeated. Intersperse these short prayers and commands as you frequently re-interview the person and evaluate what level of progress is being made in the healing process. Ask questions like, "What has happened to the pain now?" "See if you can read the sign now." "Do you still feel heat in your stomach?" "Try moving your knee now."

Remember that many of the prayers or commands for healing listed in the Bible are very short. For example: *"I am willing. Be cleansed"* (Mark 1:41). *"Little girl, I say to you 'Arise'"* (Mark 5:41). *"God, be merciful to me, a sinner!"* (Luke 18:13). *"Please heal her, O God, I pray!"* (Num. 12:13). *"In the name of Jesus Christ of Nazareth, rise up and walk!"* (Acts 3:6). *"Jesus the Christ heals you. Arise and make your bed"* (Acts 9:34).

That being said, short prayers are not always called for. We must pay attention at all times to what is going on with the person. Healing may sometimes come after an extended time of prayer or after many prayers or after several prolonged periods of praying. Short prayers can help you immediately evaluate success or discern measurable progress, but are not a one-stop formula. Always follow the leading of the Holy Spirit.

Persistence

Do not give up because one strategy or method does not seem to be working. Listen and be persistent! If you try one kind of prayer or command and get results, but do not see complete healing, then continue. Be sure to explain why you are repeating yourself. For example, perhaps you are praying for John's healing, and he is expecting you to pray only once for the condition and then stop. He might think that if there is no progress after your first prayer attempt, nothing is going to happen and he should just give up. He might ask you to stop praying and start to leave. Encourage him to stay so that you can continue to pray. Then pray as long as God seems to be improving his condition, or as long as the Holy Spirit gives you different ways to pray for him. This is the time for persistence. If healing has partially come and then seems to stop, ask him to wait for a few minutes and then resume praying and see whether another wave of healing comes.

Manner and Style of Prayer

It is not necessary to pray out loud all the time. If you prefer, tell the person that you may be praying silently at times. As long as you have your hand on the person's arm, maintain a posture of prayer—whether quietly or out loud.

People who are familiar with certain faith techniques might try to tell you, "I am healed in Jesus' name!" Confessions of faith are good, however, it is important to have an accurate measurement of what kind of progress is actually taking place in their body in order to know how to proceed. Inform people up front that you do not want them to tell you they are healed or are feeling better if that is not the case. On the other hand, encourage them to be very vocal with you, informing you of every sign of improvement throughout the prayer ministry.

People also need to know that they will not always feel something as God's healing power is released in their bodies. While this does happen, it is not always the case. There are instances where a person has been partly or completely healed without feeling anything at all. The person may not even realize that healing has actually taken place until they begin to use the affected body part. If the person does something he could not do before or that caused pain before, then they can evaluate whether the prayer thus far has made a measurable difference to their condition.

Watch as You Pray

It is very helpful to pray with your eyes open. We must continually look for signs that God is at work in the person receiving prayer and be open to cues from the Holy Spirit. Some of these signs can include fluttering eyelids, trembling, and perspiration. If you are not used to praying with your eyes open, this will require some adjustment and practice, however, it is absolutely worth it because you will be able to see what God is doing and pray more effectively based on how the Holy Spirit is touching the person you are praying for.

Continue to Pray in the Manner that Leads to Progress

I have mentioned this before however I am including it here again because it is one of the keys to effective prayer ministry. It is important for you to recognize what works and what God is using to bring noticeable change, be it major or minor. Pray based on what is working, and when that method of prayer ceases to be effective, ask the Holy Spirit for a new strategy.

Use Your Normal Tone of Voice

This is not the time to try to sound extra-spiritual by shouting or praying loudly in tongues. Such practices will not increase your effectiveness; in fact, they tend to be off-putting to the people you are praying for. The goal is to make praying for the sick a normal part of everyday life. With this in mind, *be normal* as you are praying. You do not need to manufacture any kind of experience for the person you are praying for. Don't preach, don't give advice, and don't prophesy—*just pray*. Trust the results to God. Your job is to step out, take the risk, and pray for the sick.

STEP FOUR: RE-INTERVIEW AND CONTINUE PRAYING

If after going through these first three steps, you do not seem to be making any progress, consider interviewing the person again. Possible questions might include:

"Would you try again to remember whether anything significant happened within six months or so of the beginning of this condition?" (Some event may require forgiveness that the person may have forgotten or may have been unwilling to disclose.)

"Do any other members of your family have this condition?" (If so, perhaps there is a generational spirit affecting several members of the family.)

"Do you have a strong fear of anything?" (Fear can be a cause of many physical and spiritual problems, and it sometimes interferes with healing.)

"Is anyone in your family a member of the Freemasons or Eastern Star?" (Association with Masonic or other occult organizations is particularly likely to impede healing. Some of these seem more innocent and innocuous than others, but they are all demonically influenced.)

"Has anyone ever cursed you or your family that you know of?" (If so, you can lead them in a simple prayer to break the curse by renouncing and revoking it.)

"Have you had other accidents?" (If the person is accident-prone, consider whether he is under a curse.)

"Have you ever participated in any kind of occult game or practice?"

God can and does still heal in spite of hindrances. If you are not seeing any progress in the person you are praying for, it is time to reevaluate.

DETERMINE IF AN AFFLICTING SPIRIT IS CAUSING THE CONDITION

If the person reports that the pain has moved to a different place in their body or has increased, it signals the likely presence of an afflicting spirit. Do not allow this to discourage you at all. In fact, if you identify the presence of an afflicting spirit, be encouraged. This means you know exactly how to deal with the issue at hand. Simply command the afflicting spirit to leave in the name of Jesus. You might pray with more intensity but not louder. Remember, volume does not equal authority. For example, you could pray, "In the name of Jesus, I break the power of this afflicting spirit and command it to leave Susan's body!" If the condition has existed for a long time, or if it is a condition that resists medical treatment, such as cancer, diabetes, Parkinson's, AIDS, etc., consider that there is likely to be a spirit causing the condition or resisting healing, and command it to leave. Here is another example of how to pray: "In the name of Jesus, I command any spirit of arthritis to leave this woman!"

When expelling a spirit of infirmity, an afflicting spirit, or a spirit of a particular condition, a simple prayer may be enough. If you find yourself in a situation that requires deliverance or extensive spiritual ministry, I encourage you to considering the following options: bring the person to an appropriate leader in the church who is qualified in deliverance ministry, and-or recommend helpful resources on deliverance and freedom from demonic torment.[2]

INNER HEALING

Often I find that a person who requests prayer for a physical problem is also in need of emotional healing from past hurts and wounds. These can be the results of trauma, physical or emotional abuse, perceived or real rejection, disappointments, fears, perceived or real inadequacies, and so on. These hurts and wounds often become strongholds, preventing people from experiencing deliverance and complete healing, as they are built up over long periods of time.

Let me give you some examples to help you recognize when inner healing might be necessary.

- In some cases, physical healing cannot fully be realized until a person confronts inner wounds. Once the interior issues have been appropriately dealt with, you will notice that the physical healing process often begins.

- Sometimes, even when people seem to receive physical healing, it might still be necessary for them to undergo emotional healing.

- You will encounter some people who believe that their afflictions are strictly physical, or even demonic, when in fact what they really need is inner healing.

In these cases, you should by all means take time to pray for someone's inner healing. To do so effectively, you must follow the leading of the Holy Spirit. Also, during the interview, I encourage you to keep your ears open for any language the person uses that would suggest the need for inner healing, as this will help you pray specifically and with confidence.

If the people you are praying for do *not* open up about any inner healing issues during the interview process, and you sense that such is necessary, inquire gently about any inner hurts that might be interfering with the manifestation of physical healing. Circumstances permitting, take the time to understand the situations to the best of your ability. Even a general knowledge of what the person is going through can be helpful.

There may also be cases where time is limited and you are not able to address the specific hurts that the person is going through. If you feel led, consider scheduling another ministry session with the person.

While you are praying for inner healing, pray for each specific hurt in the same way you would pray for each specific physical ailment. Francis MacNutt says that specificity is very important when praying for inner healing. This is why it is appropriate for you to follow-up with the person being prayed for from time to time, asking if the Holy Spirit is revealing anything else to them that they want prayer for. You want to be as specific as possible when acknowledging these internal hurts so you can help the person experience measurable results in these areas.

Create a safe environment so that the person can experience the healing power of God touching them in a deep, emotional place. In the same way that you will notice specific evidences of physical healing on a person's body—shaking, trembling, sweating, vibrating, and heat—there are also manifestations that accompany inner healing. These include weeping, laughing, shaking, etc. You might notice some crossover between the evidences of physical and inner healing.

Allow the person to weep. Speak encouragement over them. Let God's love, comfort, and consolation flow through you to that individual. Remember, the Holy Spirit *in you* wants to bring healing to that person physically and emotionally. When emotions are strong, it is often helpful to ask Jesus to speak to the person, or to show them how Jesus sees their situation. You may know other effective methods of praying for inner healing, or be interested in learning more. There are many excellent resources available.[3]

MINISTRY TO A PERSON WHO IS UNDER MEDICAL CARE

Sometimes people taking medication for conditions such as diabetes, asthma, arthritis, heart disease, etc., believe they have been healed when you pray for them. These individuals might think that they can immediately stop using their medication. You must instruct them to continue using their medication after ministering to them, even if they believe they have been healed.

For example, maybe you are praying for Scott to be healed of his asthma. Scott has been using an inhaler and has been on asthma medication since he was a child. Even if Scott feels as though he has been healed after your prayer session, strongly encourage him to go back to his doctor first before making any medication-related decisions.

On occasion, you will find yourself ministering to people who are consulting with a counselor or psychiatrist. This is not a significant problem if you are praying for a physical ailment, such as a broken limb or back pain. However, if you find that healing for emotional problems is indicated, you should ask the person for approval from a doctor or counselor before continuing your session. This is especially important if the person is using medication.

MINISTERING TO A PERSON WITH MULTIPLE PROBLEMS

Often in the course of prayer ministry you will be confronted with a person who is in need of prayer for more than one issue. Going back and forth, from one problem to another, can be distracting. Begin by praying for one condition. As a general rule, it is better to finish praying for one condition before starting to pray for another unless the Holy Spirit directs you differently. The person's faith for healing will increase if one healing is complete before moving on to the next.

If Sandy has a broken foot and diabetes, I encourage you to start praying for the broken foot first. This condition is smaller in scope and the results are often instantly measurable. As she is able to move her broken foot, the pain disappears, and healing manifests, Sandy's faith will increase. Perhaps going into the prayer session, Sandy was not entirely convinced that God could heal her diabetes—the larger of the two conditions. But now, after experiencing God's healing power in her foot, her faith for healing from diabetes has increased.

Do not get too locked into a formula here. While it is important to pray for one condition at a time, always following the leading of the Holy Spirit, if you are praying for Bob's sinus infection and his bad foot begins to tingle, stop praying for the sinus condition and pray for the foot. Bless what God is doing and pray in cooperation with what He is doing. Go back to the sinus infection only when you have finished praying for the foot or as you sense the presence of God manifesting in the area of sinuses.

PRACTICAL TIPS

Here are some practical tips to consider while praying for the sick:

- If possible, always use a catcher. A person may fall down even though you are praying only for a physical healing. If you don't have a catcher, have the person sit down or stand against a wall so that they cannot fall. Also consider having the person stand in front of a chair so that if they become weak, they can settle into the chair.

- If the person falls down, pray for a few moments longer and then assess the level of healing that has taken place. (Ask evaluative questions like, "How is the pain now?" or "Try moving your neck now," etc.)

WHEN TO STOP PRAYING

Here are some signs that you should stop praying:

- The person is completely healed.

- The person wants you to stop; he or she may be tired or simply feel you should stop.

- The Holy Spirit tells you it is time to stop.

- You are not given any other way to pray and you are not gaining ground.

STEP FIVE: POST PRAYER SUGGESTIONS

When the prayer time has ended, it is good to send the person away with some post prayer suggestions.

Encourage the Person's Walk with the Lord

For some people, scriptural passages are extremely meaningful and encouraging. In fact, a specific Bible verse might prove to be the anchor they stand on while believing for their healing to completely manifest. Ask the Holy Spirit for direction. He may give you a specific Scripture reference to share with the person.

Lifestyle Adjustment

If a condition resulted from occult experiences or habitual sin, suggest tactfully that a change in lifestyle may well be needed to avoid a recurrence of the condition. The key is presenting this in a sensitive way that is not judgmental or condemning. Inform the person that a lifestyle change has nothing to do with the love of God, but rather with repositioning them to experience God's freedom, healing, and wholeness. God loves the person no matter what; however, there are certain choices we need to make that position us to enjoy God's blessing and abundant life.

Faith for Healing

If the person is not healed or not completely healed, do not accuse them of a lack of faith for healing or of sin as the cause. If the person you pray for makes this evaluation on their own, encourage them as you work through this process with them. The " is not enough faith" approach is spiritually damaging and has resulted in many people rejecting healing ministry. It does not produce the fruit of compassion in a person's life, so do not go there. Encourage them to understand the necessity of rejecting this approach.

Persevere in Prayer

If there is little or no evidence of healing, encourage the person to continue to seek healing prayer. They should also continue to persevere in prayer if their healing is only partially complete. Encourage them to come back for more prayer after the next meeting, etc. Remind them that sometimes healing is a process, and that sometimes it occurs only after a number of prayers for healing have been offered. Remember, your job is to pray for healing and God's job is to heal the sick.

Fight to Keep Your Healing

Remind the person you are praying for not to be surprised if they experience a spiritual attack after receiving their healing. Help them to be prepared to resist it, as Scripture instructs (see James 4:7). If symptoms start to recur, tell the person to command the symptoms to leave in Jesus' name, using His authority. If a bad habit is involved, they might be tempted, for a short time, to recommence the habit. If they begin to fall back into a bad habit or sinful activity, encourage quick repentance.

Love! Love! Love!

In 1 Corinthians 16:14, the apostle Paul reminds us, *"Let all that you do be done with love."* As a minister of healing, do everything in love. Even if the person does not get healed, it is very important that they experience the love of God through you.

CLOSING THOUGHTS ON THE FIVE-STEP PRAYER MODEL

I want to finish this chapter with the same reminder that I opened with: Do not let yourself become locked into one model. Remember, the five-step prayer model is designed to help you get started as you pray for someone, and can be particularly helpful to those who are just beginning in the ministry of healing prayer. But God will never fit into a box. As helpful as this model can be, it will actually become a disservice if you begin to trust the model more than actively listening to the Holy Spirit's voice.

NOTES

1. See Randy Clark, *Ministry Team Training Manual* (Mechanicsburg, PA: Apostolic Network of Global Awakening, 2004).

2. Here are some books on deliverance I strongly recommend: Pablo Bottari, *Free in Christ: Your*

Complete Handbook on the Ministry of Deliverance (Lake Mary, FL: Charisma House, 2000); Francis MacNutt, *Deliverance from Evil Spirits: A Practical Manual* (Grand Rapids, MI: Chosen, 1995); and Randy Clark, *The Biblical Guidebook to Healing and Deliverance* (Lake Mary, FL: Charisma House, 2015).

3. I recommend the following books on inner healing: John Loren Sandford and Mark Sandford, *Deliverance and Inner Healing* (Grand Rapids, MI: Chosen, 1992); John Loren and Paula Sandford, *Transforming the Inner Man: God's Powerful Principles for Inner Healing and Lasting Life Change* (Lake Mary, FL: Charisma House, 2007); and Chester and Betsy Kylstra, *Biblical Healing and Deliverance: A Guide to Experiencing Freedom from Sins of the Past, Destructive Beliefs, Emotional and Spiritual Pain, Curses and Oppression* (Bloomington, MN: Chosen Books, 2003).

PART 4

TESTIFY

Chapter 10

TESTIMONY AND HEALING

While the principles found in the five-step prayer model and other models are effective tools, they must be married with testimony. This is why I tell so many stories while I am teaching. Testimony and teaching must go hand in hand. If we have all teaching without testimony, we can profoundly convey a biblical concept, but it is easy for our listeners to put those concepts somewhere in the future rather than in the "now," today. The other extreme is to teach from stories and testimonies only, never laying a solid biblical foundation for Jesus, who is the One our stories and testimonies reveal.

TESTIMONIES BRING SCRIPTURE TO LIFE

When we share biblical concepts without sharing living examples of those concepts, it becomes easy to see the concepts as something that happened "back then," or will happen "one day" in the future instead of something that can happen now. We can easily get caught up in a "but you never know with God" frame of mind that is contrary to Scripture. Testimonies stir up faith to believe that the stories found in the Bible can become a living reality in someone's life today.

TESTIMONY AND TEACHING MUST GO HAND IN HAND.

Testimony is often a lost art in the contemporary church. When we think of the word *testimony*, our thinking tends to be limited to someone's salvation story. Even though this is one expression of a testimony, it is not the only expression. Ultimately, testimony is designed to bring the Word of God to life.

We are not adding anything to the Bible with a testimony—testimony does not replace the timeless words of Scripture. Quite the opposite, in fact. When we share what God has done in our life, we are giving a living, real-life illustration of how Scripture is reliable, applicable, and relevant for today.

Before we study testimony as a term, let's consider what most Christians think of when they hear the word *testimony*.

THE SALVATION TESTIMONY

It is correct to think that testimony bears witness to a dynamic spiritual reality. This is why we describe the process of evangelism as "witnessing." We are giving witness to the power of the Lord Jesus Christ to save sinners—a transformation that we, the redeemed, have personally experienced. As we give witness, we share our personal testimonies of how Jesus saved us. The goal is for our salvation witness to stir faith in those listening so that they can believe the same Jesus who brought life and salvation to us can do the same for them.

While the story of our conversion is an important testimony, there are other stories God has given us that are designed to release faith for healing.

WHEN WE SHARE WHAT GOD HAS DONE IN
OUR LIFE, WE ARE GIVING A LIVING, REAL-LIFE
ILLUSTRATION OF HOW SCRIPTURE IS RELIABLE,
APPLICABLE, AND RELEVANT FOR TODAY.

TESTIMONIES OF GOD'S POWER AND HEALING

In the same way that we share our salvation testimonies, we must also share the mighty works of God in our lives. Just like a salvation testimony has the ability to charge an atmosphere with faith for salvation, miracle testimonies infuse an atmosphere with faith for healing.

Let's go back to the salvation example for a moment and consider its parallel application for healing stories. When someone shares a powerful salvation testimony in the presence of people who are not yet Christians, the goal is for that testimony to work with the Holy Spirit in convicting hearts, drawing people to Jesus. Ultimately, it is not the story that saves; it is the regenerating work of the Holy Spirit. Our desire is simply for people to hear a relatable testimony and believe that "if God could save him, in his condition, his utter hopelessness, his sin and depravity, then God can also save me." Salvation testimonies release faith for salvation; healing testimonies release faith for healing. God is no respecter of persons (see Acts 10:34).

CLAIM THE TESTIMONY

I want us to briefly look at some different purposes for testimony. We will conclude by walking through several live case studies of people who have been supernaturally healed. My goal is not to simply tell you what a testimony is—I want you to experience its power for yourself. When you read some of these incredible stories, both in this chapter and in the chapters to come, I believe your faith will be ignited to believe God for greater things. Also, as you share these testimonies with those in need of healing, you can help build their faith as well.

You might think you are disqualified from sharing testimonies because you personally do not have a healing testimony. Again, God has removed every barrier for your disqualification. You may not have a healing story, but I do. Take mine. Claim these testimonies as your own. If you are praying for someone, feel free to share one of my stories from this book with them. They all accomplish the same goal—building faith to believe God for healing.

Use what you have access to. Draw "living water" from whatever well is available. If you have a personal healing testimony, or if you know someone who has been healed (a family member or a friend), or you can remember a story from this book, use them all. Just be honest and authentic. I'm not encouraging you to lie about the stories, replacing my name with yours. You do not need to pretend to be Randy Clark to be successful in this. It's not about my name or your name—it's about Jesus! Trust the Holy Spirit to use these stories to build faith in those who need healing. At day's end, whether you have a healing testimony or not, you actually have access to the ultimate treasure of testimony—Scripture. Every testimony in the Bible is your inheritance. This is why the psalmist declared, *"I have inherited Your testimonies for-ever, for they are the joy of my heart"* (Psalm 119:111 NASB).

Every testimony in the Bible is your inheritance.

As a believer in Jesus, you have inherited the testimonies of the Lord. God has made them available to you because you are a part of His family! Go through the Gospel accounts and read what Jesus and the disciples did. When you are praying for someone, try to find an example in Jesus' ministry where He prayed for a similar condition. Share that story with the person you are praying for. Be specific. This makes it personal.

Chapter 11

THE PURPOSE AND POWER OF TESTIMONY

～～

One of the most relevant passages of Scripture that describes the power of testimony is Psalm 78. This psalm gives us foundational reasons why testimony is so important. It is through testimony that we share God's mighty works and his awesome power.

TESTIMONY ENCOURAGES PRAISE

Give ear, O my people, to my law; incline your ears to the words of my mouth. I will open my mouth in a parable; I will utter dark sayings of old, which we have heard and known, and our fathers have told us. We will not hide them from their children, telling to the generation to come the praises of the Lord, and His strength and His wonderful works that He has done (Psalm 78:1-4).

As we faithfully tell emerging generations about the mighty works of God that we have seen, we are inviting them into praise. Stories of God's strength and power incite praise because they confront people with the reality of God in their everyday life. He is not a concept. He is not a force. He is not distant and detached from humanity.

Creator God is not some watchmaker who wound everything up only to let it run by itself. He is involved, and one of the ways that God demonstrates His active involvement in the earth is through healing. When we share testimonies of Jesus' healing power, we are representing the very nature of God. Such a representation cannot help but stir up a climate of praise, thanksgiving, and worship in the hearts of people.

TESTIMONY INTRODUCES PEOPLE TO HOPE

For He established a testimony in Jacob, and appointed a law in Israel, which He commanded our fathers, that they should make them known to their children; that the generation to come might know them, the children who would be born, that they may arise and declare them to their children, that they may set their hope in God... (Psalm 78:5-7).

Testimonies expose people to new possibilities. Maybe someone has never heard that God heals people today. When you open your mouth and share the miracle stories of God's supernatural healing power, you are bringing hope to the hopeless. You may not know what conditions are represented in an audience, or what disease someone is struggling with. Sometimes the Lord will open these specifics up to you through words of knowledge and prophetic insight. However, when you do not have prophetic clarity, you always have the testimony. Your stories expose people to new possibilities of healing, deliverance, and freedom that might have been completely off their personal radar. This is how the testimony helps people to put their faith in God.

STORIES OF GOD'S HEALING POWER ARE WONDERFULLY CONFRONTATIONAL.

TESTIMONY KEEPS US CLOSE TO GOD

...and not forget the works of God, but keep His commandments; and may not be like their fathers, a stubborn and rebellious generation, a generation that did not set its heart aright, and whose spirit was not faithful to God (Psalm 78:7-8).

As we talk about what God is doing, we are ever reminded that God is real. He is involved and active. It is easy to live disobediently to a God whom we acknowledge as a mere concept at worse, or a cosmic clockmaker at best. Either way, God would not be present in the here and now.

Stories of God's healing power are wonderfully confrontational. They set before us the imminence of our God. He is truly among us. In response to His nearness, we live differently, we think differently, and we act differently. This kind of thinking is not motivated by religious pressure, for religion comes in when God goes out. When we view God as strictly up in heaven, waiting to either bring us up there, or coming down to earth at the end of the age, we are attempting to use religion to explain and manage our Christian life.

WHEN WE KEEP THE WORKS OF THE LORD IN FRONT US THROUGH STORIES AND TESTIMONY, WE HAVE A CONSTANT SOURCE OF COURAGE TO DRAW FROM.

TESTIMONY GIVES US SUPERNATURAL COURAGE

The children of Ephraim, being armed and carrying bows, turned back in the day of battle. They did not keep the covenant of God; they refused to walk in His law, and forgot His works and His wonders that He had shown them (Psalm 78:9-11).

The children of Ephraim were armed and seemingly ready for battle, but Scripture tells us that they turned back and retreated. The reason? Ultimately, *"they forgot what He had done—the great wonders He had shown them, the miracles*

He did for their ancestors on the plain of Zoan in the land of Egypt" (Ps. 78:11-12 NLT).

Conversely, when we keep the works of the Lord in front us through stories and testimony, we have a constant source of courage to draw from. When you come against sickness, either in your own body or in someone else's, testimonies empower you to go into battle with confidence. When you keep the track record of God's mighty works in front of you, you will be able to measure whatever you are coming against with the history of God's faithfulness. If He healed, then He will heal again. If He delivered in the past, then His arm is not short to save today.

WHEN YOU KEEP THE TRACK RECORD OF GOD'S MIGHTY WORKS IN FRONT OF YOU, YOU WILL BE ABLE TO MEASURE WHATEVER YOU ARE COMING AGAINST WITH THE HISTORY OF GOD'S FAITHFULNESS.

It is impossible for me to fully convey the power of testimony. One of the greatest revelatory teachers on this subject is Bill Johnson of Bethel Church.[1] He continually witnesses the domino effect of testimony in his ministry and church. If anyone knows about the inheritance of testimony, it is Bill. Time after time he has seen God heal people and thus produce incredible healing stories. Based on the Lord's leading, Bill will share these testimonies as he travels around the world.

One of the most remarkable things to observe in Bill's ministry is the repeatability of God's healing power based on the testimonies he shares. Bill will share how God healed a certain condition in a certain meeting or situation some time ago. Maybe the healing took place five years ago or five months ago. It really doesn't matter. All that matters is faithfully sharing the stories of what God is doing. As Bill shares testimonies of healings, those healings are actually repeated right before his eyes. In some cases, it seems like telling the story escalates the level of faith in the room. In other, more bizarre cases, it would almost appear that the testimony itself carries inherent, supernatural power to produce the miracle. As the stories leave Bill's mouth, the words go forth and start to reproduce the healing miracles he is talking about... often in real time!

IF YOU WANT TO CREATE A CULTURE OF HEALING IN YOUR LIFE OR YOUR CHURCH, YOU MUST TALK ABOUT WHAT JESUS HAS DONE.

It is time to start telling the stories of God's miracle-working power once again! If you want to create a culture of healing in your life or your church, you must talk about what Jesus has done. Share your own testimony and be sure to talk about what God is doing in other people's lives as well. Any time you hear of somebody in your church being healed, tell people about it. It is your testimony too, and as people are talking about what Jesus is doing, this constant sharing will create faith.

As we conclude the teaching portion about testimony, I want us to look at Hebrews 13:8 and Acts 10:34 for a moment.

These statements of truth are foundational for understanding and sharing testimony. For many of us, the passage in Hebrews will be very familiar: *"Jesus Christ is the same yesterday, today, and forever"* (Heb. 13:8). Earlier in Hebrews, we actually see God Himself speaking to Jesus, saying, *"You remain the same, and Your years will never end"* (Heb. 1:12).

JESUS IS ETERNALLY UNCHANGING

If Jesus is the same yesterday, today, and forever, this means that God the Father is, by default, unchanging too. It may seem strange that I have to clarify this since God and Jesus are the same. However, there are those who seem to think that Jesus represents one aspect of God, while the God revealed in the Old Testament is like another deity entirely. It does not work like that. Jesus is eternally unchanging, and thus God Almighty is eternally unchanging too. He said it Himself, *"For I am the Lord, I do not change"* (Mal. 3:6). The psalmist wrote of God, *"But You are the same, and Your years will have no end"* (Ps. 102:27). Just take this moment to firmly establish the truth in your heart that God does not change, and that the One who is eternally steadfast is also eternally good.

IF JESUS IS THE SAME YESTERDAY, TODAY, AND
FOREVER, THIS MEANS THAT GOD THE FATHER IS,
BY DEFAULT, UNCHANGING TOO. JESUS DOES NOT GO
AROUND CHANGING HIS MIND ABOUT WHO HE IS. HE
HAS ALWAYS BEEN GOOD AND WILL ALWAYS BE GOOD.

Remember, *every good gift and every perfect gift is from above, and comes down from the Father of lights, with whom there is no variation or shadow of turning"* (James 1:17). Paul reminds us that *"the Son of God, Jesus Christ, who was preached among you by us—by me and Silas and Timothy—was not Yes and No, but in Him it has always been Yes"* (2 Cor. 1:19). In other words, Jesus does not go around changing His mind about who He is. He has always been good and will always be good. The psalmist proclaims, *"For the Lord is good; His lovingkindness is everlasting and His faithfulness to all generations"* (Ps. 100:5 NASB).

NOTE

1. For a more in-depth study of testimony, and to read many stories of how testimonies contributed to building atmospheres of faith and releasing God's power, I recommend *Releasing the Spirit of Prophecy* by Bill Johnson (Shippensburg, PA: Destiny Image, 2014).

Chapter 12

THREE HEALING TESTIMONIES

*For the testimony of Jesus is
the Spirit of Prophecy*
—Revelation 19:10 NIV)

For your faith to be strengthened, you must constantly expose yourself to the testimony of what God is doing. In this chapter I am going to share three healing testimonies that I feel certain will strengthen your faith for healing.

In a world inundated with bad news, it is easy for us to get a skewed perspective. We start to focus on what God is *not* doing instead of how He *is* moving. This is dangerous because it opens the door for discouragement. All of us have disappointments at times in our life. Disappointment is actually a significant part of healing ministry. But the key is not allowing disappointment to reshape our theology. We cannot reduce our theology to the level of our experience, when our present experience is lower than biblical theology. Regard-less of what you experience, the Word of God must set the standard for what you believe. A sign of discouragement is an altered theology.

May the following three stories help orient your perspec-tive to focus on what God is doing. Remember, the same Jesus who brought healing in these stories desires to heal the sick today...*through you*. Claim these testimonies as your own!

WE CANNOT REDUCE OUR THEOLOGY TO THE LEVEL OF OUR EXPERIENCE, WHEN OUR PRESENT EXPERIENCE IS LOWER THAN BIBLICAL THEOLOGY.

CLASSICALLY TRAINED DANCER HEALED IN SAO PAULO

In 2011, I was in Brazil with a Global Awakening mis-sion team. We had been ministering in several churches in the Sao Paulo area and we had seen God moving in a mighty display of His glory as many were healed. A young woman came to one of the services in need of healing. She was in her twenties. Tall and slender, she was a classically trained dancer, but her career had been cut tragically short by an unfortunate accident.

She had been riding on a scooter when one of her ankles became entangled in the spokes of the rear wheel, resulting in a serious injury to the soft tissue. She sustained a huge gaping wound all the way to the bone, extending down the back of her leg to the base of her ankle. Doctors had been treating her for fifteen years but were unsuccessful in bringing healing.

This young woman was facing amputation of part of her leg when she came to the healing service. With great expectation for healing she received prayer, and God began to heal her. She had only been able to walk with crutches when she came to the service, due to the fact that her Achilles' tendon had been shortened because of the accident, and she had an open wound on the bottom of her leg that was large enough to put a golf ball into. But as God healed her ankle, she was able to walk unassisted. Visible signs of healing were evident as the gaping hole in her leg began to close up. We stood in awe at the glory of God on display that day.

SIGHT RESTORED AND BAPTISM

Years ago, when I was a pastor, there was a season when our church met in a school because we did not yet have a church building. As we were worshiping one day, I kept hearing the word "abortion, abortion, abortion, abortion" repeating in my head. I finally spoke out and said, "I think there is someone here who has had an abortion, and God wants to forgive you."

Now there was a woman named Sarah who had just started attending our church. I knew her story pretty well. I knew that she had been gang-raped and that she was a prostitute and an alcoholic. She had two children out of wedlock. I realized how damaged she was the first time she came to a small group. Somebody reached out to touch her and she said, "If you touch me I'll hit you. Don't you dare touch me! I don't want to be touched. I don't like to be touched."

Sarah was an interesting person. Hardened by a life of abuse, she had tried to go to church but met with rejection. One day she and her son went to a little church near their home. As she rounded a corner on her way to the bathroom, she heard two ladies in the church talking. They said, "What's our church coming to that we let that prostitute and her bastard children in here?" It was the last time Sarah went to church for many years.

The word of knowledge that the Lord gave me that morning about abortion put in motion of a series of events that eventually led to Sarah's conversion. When I gave the word of knowledge about abortion, Sarah got up and left abruptly. She did come back, but she was angry. She came to me and demanded to know, "Who told you?" She was certain someone had told me about her abortion. Eventually I was able to convince her that I had no knowledge of her abortion; that the word was from God. I told her God loved her, and that He wanted to forgive her. When she was able to embrace that truth, it marked a turning point in her life.

Sarah had been blind in one eye from her early childhood. A few weeks after the word of knowledge, one of the women in our church was driving her home. On the way home, Sarah started screaming. Suddenly she could see out of her blind eye! God sovereignly healed her eye without anyone even praying for her. She wasn't even saved but apparently God didn't mind. He wanted to pour out His love and grace upon her, and that is exactly what He did.

Soon after her eye was healed, she came to be baptized. She repented and said, "I've given my life to Jesus. I want to be baptized." I noticed that she really looked very round up front, and I was afraid she was pregnant again. I didn't want to say anything to her because of all that she had been through. She had just been saved, and the blood of Jesus had washed her past away. My attitude was, "We will love her through this— no matter what. We will help her keep her baby."

So I baptized her. She came to me later, very excited. "Look at this," she said, and pulled her slacks out indicating that there was plenty of room in the waistline. "I had to wear these bigger pants. I was supposed to have a hysterectomy tomorrow. I had lots of tumors in my abdomen. When you baptized me the tumors disappeared and now my abdomen is flat." I realized she had been instantly healed in the baptismal water!

God performed two wonderful miracles for Sarah. She was no longer a lost and broken sinner. She was a beloved child of God, saved, set free and healed. Sarah's story is a reminder that no one is beyond the reach of God's gracious healing.

ARTERIES INSTANTLY AND SUPERNATURALLY UNBLOCKED

The third healing testimony I want to share is about a woman who received an incredible healing breakthrough in

her arteries. This is how it came about. I was at home help-
ing my wife put the dishes away one day when the artery in
the right side of my neck started throbbing. You could actually see it throbbing through the skin. I thought to myself,
"What could this be?" At this point in time I had only got-
ten words of knowledge at church. It never crossed my mind
that you could get them anywhere else.[1] I knew of a woman
who had recently shared with me that she needed surgery
for clogged arteries. Because of the throbbing in my neck,
I immediately began to think of her. About a week later,
as I was on my way to church, my artery started throbbing again.

Along with this word of knowledge I felt like I had
received a gift of faith for her healing. It was my first experience with a gift of faith. When you have a gift of faith,
you pray very differently. You know the healing is getting
ready to happen no matter what the outward circumstances
or conditions. My gift of faith was so strong at that moment
that I proceeded to tell the people with me that the woman
who needed surgery on her clogged arteries was going to get
healed, tonight! Now I never give words like that, but this
was a gift of faith.

When we got to the church, she wasn't there. I felt shamed
and disappointed. I was so discouraged that I couldn't even
get into worship that night. I had been so certain that God
was going to heal her. I found myself walking around saying,
"God, why did You do that to me? I looked stupid. I thought
You said You were going to heal her."

As I was walking around complaining to God, she walked in the door—about forty minutes late. I ran back to her, caught her at the door, and blurted out, "You're getting healed tonight!" Now, I had been taught never to say something like that to a person unless you really do have a gift of faith, because if you do say something like that and they don't get healed, they can experience great disappointment.

I took her by the arm and brought her up on stage and said, "You're getting healed tonight. Everybody, watch this!" I was so expectant of what God was going to do because the gift of faith was in operation. I prayed, "In the name of Jesus, I command these arteries to be opened." Her neck started visibly shaking for everyone to see from several feet away. I learned later that she was completely healed by the power of God that night!

These are only three stories out of a multitude that I could tell you. I hope they have stirred your faith to walk confidently in God's healing power. Perhaps you will come across people in your life where these particular stories will be applicable and relevant to their unique situations. If so, use them. As you continue to read through this book, pay attention to the different stories and testimonies. They could be particularly relevant to different people you are ministering to and when you share them, faith will rise.

NOTE

1. I later learned that you can receive words of knowledge at home too. You don't need to wait until you go to church!

PART 5

PERSEVERANCE

Chapter 13

THE AGONY OF DEFEAT

LEARNING TO PERSEVERE THROUGH DEFEAT AND DISCOURAGEMENT

Years ago, television's *ABC's Wide World of Sports* opened with dramatic sports video footage displaying the jubilation of triumph and the humiliation of failure as the announcer intoned, "The thrill of victory...and the agony of defeat!"

It is absolutely wonderful to experience the thrill of victory in healing ministry: the signs and wonders, the miracles, and the healings. Yet there is a price to be paid for an individual to press into a greater anointing for healing ministry. How do we respond to the agony of defeat? We respond by learning to press ahead and persevere despite the failures, disappointments, and pain of healing ministry.

This is where we address the difficult questions, "Why doesn't everyone experience divine healing when we pray for them?" and, "How do we keep on praying for the sick when the people we pray for don't get well?" In addressing these questions, I am not claiming to have all the answers. However, I do believe it is very important that we deal with the questions because some who have represented the healing ministry in times past have not placed much, if any, emphasis on how to persevere through disappointment.

We love the thrill of victory, and rightly so, because to witness victory is to see the manifestation of our birthright as Christians. Jesus died so that we could be healed. He also died so that we could be filled with the Holy Spirit and release the healing power of the Kingdom to others. In the following chapter, we are going to spend time focusing on the thrill of victory, but for right now I want us to look at the cost of the healing ministry and how we can actually bear its weight in our daily lives.

TO WITNESS VICTORY IS TO SEE THE MANIFESTATION OF OUR BIRTHRIGHT AS CHRISTIANS.

THE COST OF THE HEALING MINISTRY

There is a cost to pay when we pray for the sick and participate in Jesus' healing ministry. Healing is part of the cross that Jesus Himself calls us to take up as we follow His example. The fact is that healing ministry truly is costly. When you receive impartation for healing, you actually commit to embrace suffering. Again, this is not an aspect of healing ministry that is normally emphasized, but it is extremely important that we are aware of the cost and are willing to talk about it.

Jesus gave the disciples an honest context of what it meant to follow him. First, He paints a picture of His death and resurrection, where agony and defeat are both represented. Luke records:

> *And He strictly warned and commanded them to tell this to no one, saying, "The Son of Man must suffer many things, and be rejected by the elders and chief priests and scribes, and be killed, and be raised the third day"* (Luke 9:21-22).

Then He specifically tells them, *"If anyone desires to come after Me, let him deny himself, and take up his cross daily, and follow Me"* (Luke 9:23).

HEALING IS PART OF THE CROSS THAT JESUS HIMSELF CALLS US TO TAKE UP AS WE FOLLOW HIS EXAMPLE.

Our culture has done everything possible to strip the cross of its weightiness by placing it on jewelry or using it as an icon to adorn church steeples. Crosses are everywhere in our twenty-first-century culture. Perhaps this is one of the reasons so many are ill-equipped to "take up their cross daily." They have no clear idea what this looks like. For many, the cross is just something else that we "put on;" it is an addition to what we already have. We have become too familiar and

145

comfortable with the cross. Rewind to the context of Luke 9 and you will discover how uncomfortable Jesus' audience was with the words He was sharing. The cross was not an "add-on" to them. Rather, it was understood as a horrible object of suffering. Jesus' disciples knew that to "take up your cross" meant to experience personal suffering.

To follow in the footsteps of Jesus means to pick up the cross of suffering. However, the same cross that testifies of incredible suffering also represents the ministry of healing. When Jesus painted this picture of "coming after" Him, He was speaking multi-dimensionally. An essential aspect of following after Jesus is modeling His healing ministry. Jesus gave us a non-negotiable when He officially commissioned the church to carry on His redemptive work in the earth.

THE SAME CROSS THAT TESTIFIES OF
INCREDIBLE SUFFERING ALSO REPRESENTS
THE MINISTRY OF HEALING.

HEALING MINISTRY AND DISCIPLESHIP

Healing ministry is a part of discipleship. We are not to only heal the sick ourselves; we are to train others to do the same. To teach someone "all the things" that Jesus has commanded us to do, we must ensure that modern disciples of Christ carry on the ministry of healing because Jesus placed such a strong emphasis upon it. Earlier in His ministry, Jesus sent out His twelve disciples, as well as seventy-two others.

He commissioned each of them to preach the good news of the Kingdom, to heal the sick, and to cast out demons. (Matthew 10:7-8). It is as if those being commissioned in the gospel accounts were to be previews of what should become normative throughout the ages, as the Holy Spirit comes to dwell inside of every believer. Jesus told them, *"Freely you have received, freely give."* What we see in the gospel accounts are ministry exploits that Jesus *began* to do and teach (see Acts 1:1). While Jesus was physically present on earth, He was providing a blueprint for what the normal, everyday Christian life should look like. Healing is not given a place of prominence in the modern church because it is often seen as disconnected from the gospel.

Defeat does not disqualify us from continuing to accomplish Jesus' Great Commission. Oftentimes churches or ministries will uphold the ministry of healing, but then give it up when their theology is shaken because of defeat. That defeat can quickly escalate into destruction if there is no solid foundation to work from.

GOD'S TRUTH OR MAN'S EXPERIENCE?

Once I was ministering in Florence, Kentucky, at the second largest Assembly of God church in the state. I was reading from Matthew 10:2, and then got to the part about raising the dead (vs. 8). I didn't like it; it actually embarrassed me. In fact, when I reached that specific point in the text, I lowered my voice out of shame. As a result, God called me out.

The Lord spoke to me and said, "You are embarrassed by that, aren't you?" I said, "Yes, I am embarrassed by that, God. I am still struggling with seeing the sick healed, let alone the dead being raised!" I was ashamed of that passage because of my lack of experience in that area. The notion of raising the dead seemed to be on another level—one that was way beyond my grasp at that time. What happened next was one of the strongest personal rebukes that I have ever heard from the Holy Spirit. This is what He said to me: "Don't you dare lower My Word to the level of your experience. Don't you be an experience-based preacher. Do not create a theology based on your experience of *not* seeing the dead raised or people healed. Preach My Word and let people's experience rise to it."

THOSE BEING COMMISSIONED IN THE GOSPEL ACCOUNTS WERE TO BE PREVIEWS OF WHAT SHOULD BECOME NORMATIVE THROUGHOUT THE AGES, AS THE HOLY SPIRIT COMES TO DWELL INSIDE OF EVERY BELIEVER.

Needless to say, I had to make some critical adjustments in how I was presenting certain aspects of supernatural ministry. Because of the Holy Spirit's rebuke, I taught for the first time publicly on how to raise the dead. I did not teach based on my experience, but drew from the testimonies and stories of other people I knew who had raised the dead.

An experience-based theology is unstable ground to build our lives upon; it will never survive the agony of defeat. In fact, when our theology is based entirely upon what we see or do not see in our own personal experience, defeat becomes stronger than the truth of God's Word. Think about it for a moment. When we preach only what we experience—whether good or bad—then our defeats have the ability to shape our theology. Every defeat subtly adjusts what we believe about God and His truth, if we allow it to. What we believe becomes informed by our personal experience. We no longer uphold the undiluted truth of God's unchangeable standard; we present a distorted composite, where there is some truth, but where there is also some experience mixed in.

WHEN OUR THEOLOGY IS BASED ENTIRELY
UPON WHAT WE SEE OR DO NOT SEE IN OUR
OWN PERSONAL EXPERIENCE, DEFEAT BECOMES
STRONGER THAN THE TRUTH OF GOD'S WORD.

If we are not careful, this theology will end up replicating in the people we disciple. When we buy into the deception of experiential theology, a disastrous momentum can set itself up which will adversely impact future generations.

We should not present an experienced-based healing ministry in the same way that we would never encourage experience-based evangelism. Could you imagine a person giving this explanation to the leader of a church evangelism team: "I am not going to evangelize anymore because every single person I have tried to lead to Jesus has told me no"? Even worse, this same person would conclude that evangelism was not even a valid ministry since not everyone we witness to receives the gospel. Based on this experience, one would conclude that it may not be God's will to save people. This perspective is contrary to very clear statements in Scripture, revealing God's desire to bring salvation to the whole world. While this scenario sounds outlandish, this is how many Christians have treated the healing ministry.

WE CANNOT ALLOW OUR EXPERIENCE WITH DEFEAT TO DETOUR US FROM WHAT JESUS CLEARLY TOLD US TO DO.

How many of us can relate to persistent defeat when it comes to sharing our faith? In many cases, it takes repeated attempts at presenting the gospel before someone actually becomes receptive and makes a decision for Christ. The same is true for the healing ministry. We cannot allow our experience with defeat to detour us from what Jesus clearly told us to do.

What happened when I started preaching God's truth instead of my personal experience? When I taught the first time about raising the dead, a man who was present in the meeting heard those words, remembered them, and used what I shared to bring his boy back to life when he was killed in an accident a few months later. Our responsibility is simply to preach the Word of God! (See 2 Timothy 4:2 NLT.)

Chapter 14

POWER AND COMPASSION

∿∿

If we want to become more involved in healing ministry, we must pray for two things: more power and more compassion. If we get power but don't have the compassion, our ministry will not reflect Jesus'. Time after time, He was moved by compassion and the result was healing. We need both God's heart and God's power to fully continue the healing ministry of Jesus.

Join me now in praying to God for three things: "Father, I ask You to keep me humble, give me Your compassion and Your heart for the lost and the sick, and finally, give me the power of Your anointing to do something about it."

When we held our first healing workshop at my Baptist church, the man who led it said to me, "Don't say [healing] doesn't work until you have prayed for at least two hundred people, because some of you will start praying for the sick and will not see anybody healed a few times...and then you will quit. But I am telling you, do not quit or say you did not get anything until you have laid your hands on two hundred people and you yourself have prayed for them. If you will do that, I promise you will be hooked for life because you will see people get healed." This man was teaching us to persist through defeat. In order to carry the cross of Jesus, we *must* learn how to persist through defeat.

WE NEED BOTH GOD'S HEART AND GOD'S POWER TO FULLY CONTINUE THE HEALING MINISTRY OF JESUS.

REALISTICALLY ENGAGING THE MINISTRY OF HEALING

You have enjoyed some testimonies of victory. Now it is time to examine testimonies of defeat. People around the world have considered this message one of the most helpful in pursuing the ministry of healing. I believe there is freedom and liberty in these words, not because of anything I can share, but simply because we are going after some highly sensitive, often controversial matters. My goal here is not to discourage you in pursuing healing; quite the opposite, in fact. People have considered this very message encouraging because it is all about perseverance. It is about what to do when you have experienced defeat.

Defeat is the common denominator that keeps people from taking risks to pray for supernatural healing. In healing ministry we stand at a crossroads: we can go right or left. Going right (pursuing the ministry of healing) often times does not make sense, because it means continuing to do the same things we have been doing, even though we have experienced limited results. Going left, on the other hand, means adjusting our theology and, most likely, backing away from healing ministry. Sadly, going left is the popular route many choose because it is comfortable, but it is not the way of the cross. Such a message promises false comfort and faithfully delivers on powerlessness. There is no resurrection life without the suffering of the cross.

DEFEAT IS THE COMMON DENOMINATOR THAT KEEPS PEOPLE FROM TAKING RISKS TO PRAY FOR SUPERNATURAL HEALING.

Many people "sign up" for healing ministry because they are sold a bill of goods that highlights the "thrill of victory." They see the empty wheelchairs and piles of unmanned crutches. They hear testimonies of impossible situations that were supernaturally turned around by the power of God. I press toward this without apology. I believe Scripture clearly reveals healing to be God's will. I am convinced without question. The fact of the matter, however, is that not everyone we pray for is healed, either instantly, progressively, or in some cases, ultimately. We cannot keep this a secret, fearing it will harm people's faith. If anything, honesty about our failures and defeats can be quite liberating for people.

Understandably, I do not share this agony of defeat message at meetings when I am hoping to see the sick get healed. It does not build faith for healing. However, it is absolutely essential that you—a Christian who has been called and empowered to do the works of Jesus—understand this message. If you are going to pray to see people healed, you are also going to see people who do not get healed. You will weep over their heartbreaking, emotional stories. Here is a transparent admission filled with a lot of painful truth: I truly believe that I have prayed for more people who have not been healed than anyone reading this book.

IF WE STEP BACK FROM THE MINISTRY OF HEALING, WE ARE ACTUALLY DEPRIVING THE SICK. DO NOT DENY THE SICK THE CHANCE TO BE HEALED BECAUSE YOU HAVE EXPERIENCED DEFEAT.

If we quit praying for the sick because of past defeats, we rob ourselves and others of the joy and delight of future victories. It is the suffering that makes every thrill of victory absolutely glorious. I would not trade it for anything. In fact, the alternative to this cross of suffering would be a counterfeit cross. Once again, Jesus did not give us two options: Cross A or Cross B. He simply gave an invitation to take up *His* cross and follow *Him*. For us to continue in the healing ministry, we need to engage it realistically.

DEPRIVING THE SICK

While God is known to sovereignly heal people, be it in His presence or through some other kind of supernatural experience, His primary method for releasing healing is through Spirit-filled vessels. Our hands are catalysts that release God's healing power. Our words carry the weight and power of the Kingdom of God. It has nothing to do with us; it has everything to do with the Spirit inside of us and the Word of God in our mouths.

If we step back from the ministry of healing, we are actually depriving the sick. Do not deny the sick the chance to be healed because you have experienced defeat. Press on. Persevere. Go for it. Take it from me, someone who has experienced more defeat in the healing ministry than perhaps anyone else on the planet. If I had given up, I would not have been able to write the next chapter: "The Thrill of Victory." In our Christian culture, by and large, we are taught to continue sharing and preaching the gospel, leaving the results in God's hands. Let us take the same approach toward the healing ministry. Along with Jesus' power within us through the Holy Spirit, we must embrace His heart of compassion if we are to minister effectively to those who are lost, broken and hurting. Power and compassion go hand in hand. Jesus needed both to minister healing, and so do we.

Some time ago, I came across a man whose adult daughter had died. He had not prayed for a single person since her passing. He somehow blamed himself because she had not been healed. This belief was absolutely crippling to him, as it is to so many others who have experienced similar defeats—particularly those defeats that are deep and personal. This man came and listened to one of my messages. After the session he said that I gave him back the right to start praying for the sick again. From that day onward, he began to do so.

Chapter 15

LEARN TO EMBRACE
SUFFERING

Christianity has become too comfortable. When people ask "Why did this person get healed and that one didn't," or "Why did that sinner get healed while the pillar of our church died of the same condition?" you have to be able to tell them, "I don't know." To be involved in the healing ministry, you must be willing to embrace emotional suffering and be willing to say, "I don't know."

STORIES OF DEFEAT

The stories I am about to share with you will touch each of you in different ways. The common denominator is defeat. Healing did not come for the individuals involved, and every defeat was a potential invitation for me to give up.

I cannot help but think of notable healing evangelists like Aimee Semple McPherson or Kathryn Kuhlman who openly and painfully confronted defeat. Even though McPherson saw thousands healed, people would still find her weeping for all of the stretchers that came in ambulances and left in ambulances. In her book *A Glimpse Into Glory*, Kathryn Kulhman writes about weeping over those in her meetings who did not get healed. Journalists wanting an interview Kulhman would find her backstage, crying over the cancer patients and dying children who did not receive their miracles. She truly recognized the cross of the healing ministry.

IMPARTATION—BE STRENGTHENED BY THE HOLY SPIRIT

I want you to receive an impartation of compassion and perseverance as you read my stories of defeat. I am asking the Holy Spirit to touch you and to cause you to see pain and hear the cry. God said to Moses: *"I have seen the affliction of My people and I have heard their cry and I have come down to deliver them, and so I am sending you"* (Exodus 3:7-10). If Jesus Christ is the same yesterday, today, and forevermore, and if He loved to heal the sick and cast out demons, doesn't He still want to do it through His people today? The answer is "yes," but the question is, "Who can God use if not us?" The emotional pain involved in this process can't sideline us; we must become strengthened by the Holy Spirit. That is what this impartation is about. It is about inviting you to the cross of the healing ministry of Jesus Christ.

Boy without a Functioning Brain

In 1994, soon after I had received a prophetic word about being used in the healing ministry, I went to minister at a church in New Jersey. The church was round and had a balcony—there were about 700 people in attendance. We had powerful services there, but I felt specifically that the Lord told me not to preach there on Sunday morning. Instead, He sent us over to a little church where there were only about twenty people present.

After the service, a woman in her twenties came over with a little boy who was about two years old. The woman's husband had left her because the child had been born with minimal brain function. This severe birth defect meant the child was unable to communicate. The little boy would never be able to acknowledge that she was his mother. I knew this woman had come because she heard that I was speaking. She was desperately hoping that God would give her a miracle. I prayed over this child for over an hour while the mother told me how hard it was for her and what a heavy burden she carried because the father was gone. I prayed and prayed, but the little boy did not get healed that day.

Children with Birth Defects and Terminal Illnesses

I got out of the service around two or three in the afternoon, obviously carrying the disappointment of that defeat. One of the pastors from the larger church came up to me and said, "Randy, we just want you to know there have been so many healings and the faith level has gone so high that parents are going over to the institutions and getting their children to bring to the meeting tonight."

These were children who had been placed in institutions due to the severity of their birth defects. This news did not thrill me, to say the least. I felt very weighed down by the whole situation and quite overwhelmed. The place was packed when I walked into the service that night.

Boy with Destroyed Muscle Tissue

Right in front of me was a little boy, somewhere between nine and eleven years old. He had a rare disease that had destroyed all his muscle tissue. The disease was a fatal, terminal disease. He looked like a skeleton wrapped in skin because he was so skinny. As the music played, he was shaking one leg to the beat of the music. I was overwhelmed with the compassion of God. While we worshiped for forty-five minutes, I stood behind this boy and prayed for him, but he was not healed.

I used to say that nothing happened, but someone corrected me. A person told me about eight years later that this boy was still alive and no one had ever lived that long with that condition. It was as though the disease dropped right at that point—that night, as I prayed during worship. He was not healed, but something did happen.

Teenager with Hydrocephalic

As the service continued on, I taught a message on healing. Then the doors opened up in the back and in walked this mother and father in their mid to late thirties with their teenage son strapped to a gurney. They pushed the gurney up to the front as I watched from the pulpit. It was clear that this mother and father were desperate for a miracle for their son and were hoping that tonight would be his night to be healed.

The boy thrashed around on the gurney, making loud verbal noises. During the interview, I found out that he was hydrocephalic. The shunt that the doctors had put inside of him had collapsed and kinked, causing massive brain damage. He went from being normal and communicative to a spastic, no longer able to communicate intelligibly. The mom and dad looked at me with hope that God would use me to raise up and restore their afflicted son. I felt their hope. I felt their expectation. I felt the weight of their desire for God to use me. I prayed and prayed, and after a while as nothing happened, all those hopes and expectations decreased. The boy did not get healed.

All of these stories happened around the same time, back in 1994. It is amazing that I can't remember any of the ones who were healed during that time—and there were hundreds healed in those services. However, I cannot forget that teenager on the gurney, the boy who was skin and bones, and the little boy without a functioning brain.

Boy in a Wheelchair

Next, I was off to Knoxville, Tennessee. The Lord spoke to me and said, "You are not going to see people in wheelchairs healed unless you pray for them more." There were about 1,000 people in the meeting and scores, if not hundreds, were healed. "Around midnight, I saw a fourteen-year-old boy in a wheelchair. As I walked over to the boy I could smell the strong odor of urine. Now I have a very weak stomach. But I thank God that He gave me a very poor sense of smell because smells can easily make me feel sick. I thought, "What would Jesus do?" He would not be repulsed; He would push through because of His love for the boy. Therefore, I knelt down beside the boy, asked his name, and also asked what was wrong with him. He had spina bifida, with no control over his bladder. He needed a miracle, so I prayed with him.

After fifteen or twenty minutes, he looked at me and said, "You know, I am one of several adopted children in my family. Every one of us has birth defects. My sister is over there. Tonight may not be my night. I will go with you and let's go pray for my sister."

Girl with Cerebral Palsy

We made our way over to his sister, who was born with cerebral palsy. I started to pray for his sister, who was also in a wheelchair. I never try to pull people up out of a wheelchair, but I also never discourage them if they want to try and get up for themselves. The sister said, "I want to try to walk." I helped her up and we started to walk together. She would take a step and one toe would catch behind the other foot. I would reach down and pull it out while all the time praying for her healing. She took another step and the same thing happened again. This cycle continued all the way across the stage and back. She then collapsed into her wheelchair, and she was not healed.

Blind Girl

Next, I went to High Point, North Carolina, where I preached at a healing conference. During the invitation, lots of people came forward and were healed. What I specifically remember were three twelve-year-old girls—two brunettes and one blonde. I was thinking, "These girls are so full of faith." I thought maybe the blonde girl had a toothache or was having relationship problems. Then I asked her what she wanted prayer for. She looked up at me and simply said, "I am blind." Nothing looked wrong with her eyes.

Surprised, I said, "You are blind! How?"

She said, "When I was six years old, in kindergarten, I had this rare disease and lost my sight. I believe Jesus can heal me." I prayed for her during each of the three sessions, every day of the conference. I prayed for her more than anybody else during that conference. I prayed longer and longer for her every session. She came so expectantly.

I would ask her, "Is anything happening?"

She would say, "I think I am beginning to see."

"Can you see my fingers?" I would ask.

She would say, "Not yet, but I think I am beginning to see."

This happened for three days until the final session. I was praying for her and asked again, "Can you see my fingers?"

She simply said, "No." At that moment, she realized she was not being healed. This is where I made a mistake that is so common to all of us. We are all human and thus we make mistakes and errors in judgment.

My heart was so drawn to this twelve-year-old girl, probably because I had a daughter around her age. I did not use wisdom and said something to her that actually made things worse. I reached down, took her in my arms, and whispered in her ear: "Rose, I so wanted you to be able to see what a beautiful young woman you are becoming." She spun around and threw her arms around her mother's waist. She was shaking and weeping while her mom was crying. I walked away with tears running down my cheeks. That took place back in 1995, and I cannot forget her name.

A friend saw what happened and told me, "She got behind your shield." Like a doctor or nurse, when you do this type of work you must put a shield around your emotions. You want to love, but you also have to get up and do it again tomorrow. You don't want to be burned out by the emotions involved. We minister in love and compassion, absolutely, but we cannot get emotionally involved with the people we pray for. People have condemned me saying I should not have a "shield." Wait until you have prayed for about 10,000–20,000 people, and then come and tell me that. Just imagine how many people out of 20,000 do not get healed. If I became emotionally involved with each one I would quickly be spent.

That said, several years ago, Rose sent me a Christmas card with a note that said, "I'm still believing for my healing, and don't you be discouraged. You keep praying for the sick." I extend this same invitation to you. Don't get discouraged by what you don't see happening. Continue to pray for the sick, taking up your cross and following Christ. We keep praying and trust the results to the Healer.

Woman with a Head Injury

Once I went to minister at a large church in Anderson, Indiana. As I preached and the crowd stood for the invitation, I was drawn to one particular person, a very tall and handsome young man. I have learned to pay attention to these things, as they often signify what the Holy Spirit wants to do. I didn't understand why I was honed in on this individual, but I knew that something was wrong.

After the invitation, as we started praying for the sick, I walked straight over to him. When I reached the young man, I understood what was wrong. Beside him in a wheelchair sat the remains of a beautiful young bride in her twenties. She had a big concave hole in the side of her head where a portion of her skull once was. Saliva dripped down her chin. Her husband—who had vowed for better or worse, for richer or poorer, in sickness and in health—had a washcloth that he was using to wipe the saliva trickling down her chin. He was there because he desperately hoped that I would be the one God would use to restore his bride to him. I prayed and prayed, but she was not healed.

Girl with Parkinson's Disease

Next, I ministered in a church in northwest Indiana that believed in healing. I told the miraculous story of a forty-nine-year-old woman who was totally restored from Parkinson's disease. The next night, a twelve-year-old girl came forward for prayer. Her father, who had brought her, had to stand behind her to hold her up since she could not stand on her own. She wanted me to pray for her because she heard the testimony about the healing for Parkinson's. At the time, this girl at twelve years of age was the youngest person in the United States with Parkinson's. As I specifically focused and concentrated on praying for her, my team prayed for almost everyone else. I prayed for that girl during every session, thirty minutes to one hour each time. She didn't get healed.

When I was praying for her, I saw that her hope was starting to dwindle. She began to move into despair and began crying. Somebody gave her a handkerchief, and she struggled to wipe her own nose. Her mom and dad stood there, remembering the inspiring testimony I told about the woman who was healed from this debilitating disease. The girl was also remembering that story, but she left without being healed. How do you handle that without giving up? Jesus paid for our healing with his broken body, his very life. We who minister healing in His name will pay for it with our broken hearts.

Chapter 16

POWER FOR MIRACLES

One of my responses to the agony of defeat that I was experiencing was to embark on a forty-day fast, asking God to increase my anointing for healing. I was desperate. My heart was being ripped out by those defeats. In general, I am not a person who fasts and I am not religiously mandating that fasting is the only way we are to respond when we experience defeat in healing. All I know is that the experience of these failures caused me to pray, "Oh God, the anointing that I have right now is not enough. It is not enough to have an anointing for healing. All of these conditions need miracles. Something has been destroyed that must be re-created, or something is there that needs to be destroyed. It is not healing these people need—they need miracles. I need the power for miracles." On the twenty-third day of the fast a forty-nine-year-old woman was supernaturally healed of Parkinson's disease—the first miracle!

We should not let defeat *defeat* us. Instead, we must let defeat *drive* us. I let defeat drive me into a place of crying out for increase. Obviously my present level of anointing was not sufficient—I needed *more*. I did not accept this as an opportunity to feel condemned or think that God was upset with me. Likewise, you should not feel that way either. I let defeat drive me into a place of crying out to God for more anointing so that people in need could receive the miracles they so desperately desired and I so desperately longed for them to have, no matter the cost.

LET DEFEAT DRIVE YOU.

I've always been inspired by Bill Johnson's testimony of how he experienced God's increased anointing. It took place over the course of three nights. As God's power touched his body, Bill commented that he looked like a spastic lying in bed with no control over his arms and legs. During this experience, he felt like God asked, "Would you be willing to bear the stigma of being a spastic for the anointing?" Bill began to consider what people might think of him being in this condition—having no control over his legs or arms. He could see himself walking down the streets of Redding, California, trying to explain what God did to him. God was asking, "Would you be willing to bear the stigma?" And lying there, with tears running down his face, Bill responded in a way that I believe has gone on to define his ministry and church. He said, "If this is what it costs to have more, Lord, I would be willing to bear this." He meant it, and now he and the community of Bethel Church are seeing incredible healing breakthroughs on a near daily basis.

ARE YOU WILLING TO PAY THE COST TO RECEIVE THE ANOINTING, TO RECEIVE MORE, TO SERVE GOD, AND BRING HEALING AND MIRACLES TO THOSE IN NEED?

I prayed for twenty years for stroke victims before I saw the first one healed. It was the testimony of the dead raised in Mozambique that gave me a greater degree of faith to believe for the healing of stroke victims. Then within twenty-four hours we saw three stroke victims healed. I never saw an AIDS victim healed until recently, when we saw three healed in one year! It was more than twenty-five years before we saw the first blind person healed. Then, in one month, we saw twenty blind people healed. I only prayed for a few of them, while our ministry team prayed for the rest. Could you imagine what would have happened if I let negative results keep me from moving on? If I had allowed defeat to inform whether or not I continued with the healing ministry? I could have stopped!

Are you willing to pay the cost to receive the anointing, to receive more, to serve God, and bring healing and miracles to those in need?

Defeat can be a powerful influence if we do not respond to it appropriately. It was only on the other side of perseverance—in some cases, over years and even decades—that I have seen some of the greatest breakthroughs and miracles. When you genuinely believe that defeat is your cue to give up, because all you will ever experience is defeat, you are buying into deception. Scripture is filled with calls for us to persevere.

WHEN YOU GENUINELY BELIEVE THAT DEFEAT IS YOUR CUE TO GIVE UP, BECAUSE ALL YOU WILL EVER EXPERIENCE IS DEFEAT, YOU ARE BUYING INTO DECEPTION.

How many people would be willing to pray for hundreds who don't get healed in order to see a forty-nine-year-old woman who was losing her mind to Parkinson's disease totally healed and given back to her husband, or see a little boy whose nerves were gone, destroyed, and deaf, be totally restored? How many people would be willing to pray for hundreds who don't get healed to see a mother who is in her twenties dying of an inoperable brain tumor be healed by God?

Are you willing to embrace the pain and suffering in order to experience the thrill of victory? When we experience defeat do we let our hearts drift into that place where the reality of Scripture is no longer in operation, or do we become angry at the devil? I believe we must become more determined than ever to come into a place of greater anointing and breakthrough so that we do not lose anyone else to sickness. We must take an aggressive stand against diseases like cancer or leukemia, refusing to let any more succumb to disease.

Bill Johnson is intent on seeing Redding, California, become a cancer-free zone. He suffered a great defeat specifically to cancer, when his own father lost his battle with cancer. Instead of giving up, however, the Bethel community has gone after this enemy with even greater vigor and are seeing incredible miraculous victories as a result.

GOD IS CALLING US OUT BEYOND THE COMFORTABLE AND BECKONING US INTO A LIFESTYLE OF TAKING UP HIS CROSS.

GOING DEEPER

I know that God wants us all to go deeper. He is calling us out beyond the comfortable and beckoning us into a lifestyle of taking up His cross. This is God's only option because it is the only route to true fruit and victory. Everything else keeps us in a place of ultimate defeat.

There is so much more available to us. In fact, I believe the Bible's teaching that in the last days we will experience the greatest revival the world has ever seen. One of the evidences of this revival will be the restoration of healing, signs, and wonders as normative practice for the New Testament church. This is the deeper reality we are all pressing into. We will not be the lukewarm Laodicean church of Revelation 3; rather, we will be a church on fire with the Holy Spirit and His power. It will be an era of great contrast on the earth: deep darkness and glorious light. It will be a time of intense persecution that will cause the great falling away. But it will also be a time of great harvest because every time there is martyrdom, there is a release of the fire and power of the gospel. Evangelism efforts intensify. In the book of Acts, it was persecution that brought expansion to the church. The last day's church will not be recognized by its weakness, but instead by its power and boldness.

Even though you may experience defeat, you are part of an undefeated, unshakeable Kingdom. Be grounded in this identity because it will sustain you through setbacks, trials, and disappointments. We need to catch a glimpse of the bigger picture if we are going to endure through difficultly and take our place in this great last day's harvest.

THE LAST DAY'S CHURCH WILL NOT BE RECOGNIZED BY ITS WEAKNESS, BUT INSTEAD BY ITS POWER AND BOLDNESS.

As the body of Christ, we are moving into this time of awakening and revival. Haggai 2:9 says, *"the glory of this latter house shall be greater than of the former"* (KJV). We see evidences of this across the world. No longer are we just referring to prophecies; these words are actually coming to pass before our very eyes! Revival is no longer some nebulous concept that excites us, always somewhere off in the distance, prophesied to come "one day." It's here!

God is reviving His people, restoring an authentic expression of New Testament signs, wonders, and miracles in our midst. The Holy Spirit is releasing a great anointing upon the church. This is not some superficial thing. God's anointing is a call to radically follow the model of Jesus Christ. It is a summons to pick up His cross, follow Him, love as He loved, to feel as He felt, and to cry out for Him to anoint you with power for the task at hand. God wants to release another great missionary wave that He will dispatch to the four corners of the earth. These fiery missionaries will go forth with a strong commitment to healing and deliverance, recognizing that the gospel of the Kingdom comes in both proclamation and demonstration.

GOD IS REVIVING HIS PEOPLE, RESTORING AN AUTHENTIC EXPRESSION OF NEW TESTAMENT SIGNS, WONDERS, AND MIRACLES IN OUR MIDST.

These are not times for us to second-guess our commission to bring the Kingdom. If I can persevere through defeat, so can you. We have received the same Holy Spirit. The same empowering presence of God that has sustained me through decades of both thrilling victory and agonizing defeat will do the same for you too. He is no respecter of persons. Draw from the deep well of His strength and ability. It is not optional; we must do this for the times we are living in.

I want to encourage you to ask for a fresh baptism of the Holy Spirit. Even if you have already received the "baptism of the Spirit," I believe the Bible makes it clear that there are multiple baptisms to be experienced. Even though you are baptized into Christ at salvation and you receive water baptism to identify with Christ's death, burial, and resurrection, there is still more. In fact, there is even more than a one-time baptism in the Spirit, where you spoke in tongues for the first time, fell down, prophesied, or had some kind of supernatural experience with God. This moment is to be celebrated, but it is not conclusive. Theologian Gordon Fees tells us to pray for a fresh baptism of the Holy Spirit to give us the power to work miracles, and the power to walk through the darkness when the miracles do not come. We should expect a lifetime of continuous, increased anointing. Press through from defeat to victory. Ask for a fresh baptism of the Holy Spirit and God will give it to you!

WE SHOULD EXPECT A LIFETIME OF
CONTINUOUS, INCREASED ANOINTING.

Chapter 17

THE THRILL OF VICTORY

FIVE PRINCIPLES FOR HEALING

In this chapter, along with testimonies of victory, I am going to give you five principles for healing. Each of these principles is true, but if you turn them into laws, they will surely backfire. The devil specializes in taking the law and beating you up with it. We must always leave room for the sovereignty of God and the work of the Holy Spirit. In fact, every one of the illustrations I use for each principle will actually contradict the principle itself, thus reinforcing that it is not an ironclad law. Mercy always triumphs over judgment. Healing is an extension of God's mercy. God will violate these principles to reveal His mercy, love, and compassion. This does not mean He is throwing out biblical truth. He is just bringing healing to pass in a manner that is outside our limited human understanding of how we thought something should happen.

#1: THE PRINCIPLE OF FAITH

The first and most important principle is the principle of faith. In Matthew 9:22, Jesus told the woman with the issue of blood, *"Take heart, daughter…your faith has healed you"* (NIV).

THE DEVIL SPECIALIZES IN TAKING THE
LAW AND BEATING YOU UP WITH IT. MERCY
ALWAYS TRIUMPHS OVER JUDGMENT. HEALING
IS AN EXTENSION OF GOD'S MERCY.

Faith that Moves Mountains

In Matthew 9:29, Jesus told two blind men, *"According to your faith let it be to you,"* and their sight was restored. It was all about faith. If you have faith, you can speak to the mountain, and it will be thrown into the sea (see Mark 11:23-24). If you have faith, you can speak to the mulberry tree, and it will be uprooted—if you have faith and do not doubt (see Luke 17:6). Jesus demonstrated this by speaking to a tree and it withered overnight (see Mark 11:20-21).

Sometimes we have difficulty with Scripture, as is often the case with that well-known passage from Mark that deals with the fig tree and the importance of faith. In this instance it is not that Scripture is so obscure that we can't understand it. The verses are quite clear. In Mark 11:22-24 Mark calls our attention to the withered tree, remembering that Jesus had cursed it, and Jesus responds by saying, *"Have faith in God. For assuredly, I say to you, whoever says to this mountain,*

'Be removed and be cast into the sea,' and does not doubt in his heart, but believes that those things he says will be done, he will have whatever he says. Therefore I say to you, whatever things you ask when you pray, believe that you receive them, and you will have them."

The real problem with this Scripture is not our inability to understand what it means. The real problem is learning to walk in the reality of what this Scripture reveals. Jesus is telling us to have extraordinary faith, beyond anything we have known before, and if we do, God will back it up. The challenge before the church is not to understand something difficult from Scripture, but to walk in the light of the truth of Scripture. Action must follow faith—understand, have faith, walk in that faith.

In Mark 11:22-24, Jesus is extending an invitation and a promise to us. It is supernatural. It is outside the realm of possibility. He is challenging us to see and live on a higher level, and this is why people try to take Bible passages that speak of the supernatural and naturalize them. We want something comfortable, not demanding. The faith that Jesus describes is demanding. It confronts us with our present condition and calls us up higher.

WHEREVER THERE IS MORE FAITH, MORE HAPPENS. WHENEVER THERE IS GREAT FAITH, GREAT THINGS HAPPEN.

Faith that Pleases God and Produces Fruit

Hebrews 11:6 says, *without faith it is impossible to please God."* Faith is nonnegotiable for the Christian. It is so fundamental to our relationship with God that apart from faith we cannot experience His pleasure. Furthermore, I believe that based upon the best advancements in medical science today, God, our Creator, created us in such a way that our bodies are hardwired to respond to faith. Because God loves us so much, He has formed us so that our bodies can and do respond to faith. The placebo effect is proof of this.

So the principle is this: Wherever there is more faith, more happens. Whenever there is great faith, great things happen. Where there are more people of faith, more things happen in that congregation than in a congregation where there is less faith. It is that simple. Jesus Himself could do no mighty deeds in Nazareth because of the unbelief of the people there (see Matt. 13:58).

IF WE WANT TO SUSTAIN A LIFESTYLE OF FAITH FOR HEALING, IT IS IMPORTANT THAT WE FEED ON FAITH.

Faith Feeds on Faith

I would rather be around people with more faith than me, than with people who have less faith than me. I do not want to be hanging around people who are questioning God. I want to hang around people who are bragging on God. Their faith stirs my faith. Their confidence in God is positively infectious. These are the kind of people who "feed" our faith. If we want to sustain a lifestyle of faith for healing, it is important that we feed on faith. One way we do this is by surrounding ourselves with people who are focused on what God is doing instead of getting hung up on what they think He is not doing.

Do not surround yourself with doubters and listen to their voices. I have learned this firsthand. As a result, I want to surround myself with people who have seen the dead raised and raised the dead. I want to be around people who have seen and done exploits for God. I want my faith to continually grow. With this in mind, I encourage you to surround yourself with people of faith. Even when your faith is being challenged, or you are struggling, or you are coming off a defeat, it is vital to have people of faith speaking hope into you. They will remind you of God's faithfulness and unchangeable nature. They will make it very difficult for you to give up because they will continue to sow faith into you.

A GIFT OF HEALING IS SIMPLY THE GRACE
OF GOD BEING MANIFESTED, THE KINGDOM
BREAKING THROUGH, MERCY TRIUMPHING OVER
JUDGMENT, AND GRACE BEING RELEASED.

Faith and Grace

Having said all of this concerning the importance of faith, I caution you not to move outside of God's grace. Beyond every principle in this chapter, the most important thing to understand is God's grace. The gift of healing is a *charisma*, from which we get the word "charismatic." *Charisma* is a Greek word that means a grace or an expression of grace. A gift of healing is simply the grace of God being manifested, the Kingdom breaking through, mercy triumphing over judgment, and grace being released.

Grace is a supernatural enablement, a divine empowerment to accomplish something. This means that our entire ministry is grace-based. John Wimber taught me this valuable lesson: When you stand praying for somebody, don't step off the rug of peace. What did he mean by that? He meant that we should stand in the place of God's grace and peace, because it is God who does the work of healing. We cannot do it.

I AM AGAINST THIS BELIEF THAT IF WE BECOME EMOTIONAL, GOD WILL BE MORE INCLINED TO MOVE THAN IF WE ARE QUIET IN OUR SPIRITS AND STANDING ON THE "RUG OF PEACE."

How do faith and grace work together? When it comes to the healing ministry, pray with confidence and speak boldly to the condition. Don't neglect the role of faith. At the same time, remember that you don't have to rev yourself up. You do not have to try to work up your spirit or your soul to make something happen. This can be the danger of being overly faith focused. The fact is that the faith we have is not even ours to begin with; it is a gift from God! In the same way that God gave you faith for salvation, this God-given faith is what you steward when it comes to praying for the sick. You can't make faith work—God does! If you try to pray for the sick by working yourself up, four things may happen: One, you get tired more quickly; two, you wear out; three, you lose your voice yelling; and four, often you will miss a word from the Lord in the midst of your emotionalism. It is that simple.

I am an emotional person. I think that emotions are good since God made emotions for us. There are toxic emotions and there are good emotions, and I am not against emotions or being emotional. If I had lived in the 1500s, I would have been called an enthusiast because I believe that God still speaks to us, and I desire to experience it all. While I am not against emotion, I am against this belief that if we become emotional, God will be more inclined to move than if we are quiet in our spirit and standing on the "rug of peace." Greater volume does not assure greater victory. Remember, it is not your effort that ultimately matters. God is just looking for faith and risk. He is looking for those who follow the principles and for those who lay down the principles for the sake of hearing His voice. Operating from this place of grace-based rest is not always easy because we so desperately want to see breakthrough.

Woman with Parkinson's

Let me share an example of how God works in spite of our level of faith. I love sharing this testimony because it reminds me of God's grace and the power of perseverance. To be honest, sometimes we just do not want to pray for people.

I have been there. This story I am about to share is a classic example of divine interruption and why we must always have our eyes set on watching what God is doing in our midst. We may have one agenda, and God might have another. This story reminds me to pursue God's agenda above my own, no matter how important I perceive my agenda to be.

During one meeting, I was very focused on impartation—primarily for the young people. Because of this focus, I directed everybody who was over twenty-nine and needed healing to go to the balcony where we had a ministry team administering healing prayer. It was the only time in a series of meetings that I planned not to pray for the sick.

I was not expecting to pray for healing for anyone. Then, Angela came up to me. She looked like she was sixty years old or older (when really, she was only forty-nine). She was shaking, and I just thought that the anointing of God was on her because there was a whole lot of shaking going on in the meeting.

She came up to me and said, "I want you to pray for me."

I said, "No, you are over twenty-nine years old, so you go on up to the balcony."

She said, "I want you to pray that I will be healed."

I said, "Well, you just go on up there, and they will pray for you."

She said, "I have already been up there and I didn't get healed, and God told me if you would pray for me I would get healed."

I found out later that she had never heard of the Toronto Blessing and never heard of Randy Clark, but when she got the flyer in the mail about the meetings I was going to hold, she felt she heard God say, "If you will go and have him pray for you, I will heal you." I did not know that at the time, so I was trying to tell her that I did not want to pray for her. She said, "No, you have to pray for me."

Sometimes it is easier just to pray for people than to argue with them. Angela continued to shake. Then she looked at me and said, "I have Parkinson's. I am in the last stages of Parkinson's disease. I am losing control of my bladder. I was in a grocery store the other day with my husband. I can't even walk without leaning on his arm because of what is going on, and I peed all over myself right in line. I was terribly embarrassed because now I am losing control of my bodily functions, my bladder and my bowels. I don't have any short-term memory left. I have a two-year-old grandson that I have never held because I shake so badly that my child is afraid I will drop my grandson. I need to be in a nursing home, and I can't afford it. I don't want to live if I have to continue living like this."

Here is where the principle of faith was violated. After hearing Angela's story, I didn't have any faith, although I did have a little compassion. So I stuck my hand out, and I was going to say, "Come, Holy Spirit" to see what He would do. As I stuck my hand out, and said, "Come..." Angela immediately hit the floor. Since she was on the floor, I thought, "Okay, now I can go pray for others." So I moved to where others were waiting and prayed over them.

While praying for these others, I continued to look where Angela was lying. She was still out. I was on the twenty-third day of the first forty-day fast I mentioned to you a while back. We had seen wonderful healings, but we were running into a lot of little children who needed more than a healing—they needed creative miracles. I was fasting and praying for a breakthrough in creative miracles.

I went over to her husband whose name was John. I asked him, "What's Parkinson's? What does it do?" He said, "It actually destroys part of the brain and the cells." He began to explain to me how the disease affects the neurological system, destroying it. He said that a person has 800 million brain cells, but his wife only had about 50,000 left. She didn't need a healing. She needed a creative miracle!

Remember, I started out not even wanting to pray for her. I did not have any faith or expectation for her healing. However, as John told me about his wife's condition, I remembered that on the way to the meeting, my worship leader's wife had started weeping uncontrollably. The gift of intercession was in operation in her. Her tears were a prayer, an expression of her emotional exhaustion. She said, "You guys keep coming home and telling me about all these miracles that you have seen, and I haven't seen one. I want to see one."

Remembering the prayer of my worship leader's wife, I went over to Angela who was still on the floor. I put my hand on her head, and I said, "I call those things that are not as though they were. God, I ask You for five hundred million—no, that's the wrong number—I need eight hundred million new brain cells." When I said that, she started squirming, grabbing her head, screaming and yelling, saying, "Oh! Oh! Oh! It hurts! My head! My head is killing me! Stop praying!"

Suffice it to say, my four years of college in religious studies and three years in seminary did not prepare me for what to do next. What do you do as God is performing a creative miracle, and the person receiving it is screaming at you? I never had a class on that one, so I got a word of wisdom. I said, "God, don't listen to her prayer! Listen to mine! More! More! More!"

Now, Angela was lying on the floor, and I was down on my knees right beside her. The music was still going on, and there were people praying everywhere. All of a sudden, after I said "More, Lord!" she became perfectly quiet. She lay there, not moving. I got down beside her and whispered in her ear, "Angela, what's happening?" She said, "I don't feel anything. I don't hear anything. All I know is that you're here, Jesus is here, and John is here."

Then she lifted up her right arm—a simple gesture, nothing exciting. I was incredibly happy though, because I knew what she was doing. For the first time in years she was looking at her hand and it wasn't shaking. Then, performing the simple test for Parkinson's, she began to touch her index finger to her nose with her left arm. Then her husband brought her a cup of water, which she proceeded to drink with no difficulty, no longer unable to swallow. God was healing her!

Next she stood up, and she asked if she could go on stage. I figured God had healed her, so she was queen for a day and she could do whatever she wanted! She walked right up on the stage in front of everyone. By this time, it was around midnight, and I remembered John Wimber's teaching that the greatest miracles and healings often happen late at night, because the most desperate people stay, determined to be prayed for.[1]

Up on stage, Angela grabbed her husband's hand and started shaking it. She said, "Look at this! I am shaking my husband's hand. Look at that! We have been spending two hundred eighty dollars a month on my medication. Just think what John and I are going to do with that money! I am going to go home and hold my two-year old grandson for the first time.

Then she asked for a piano. We didn't have one but we had a keyboard and I directed her to it. As she sat down and began to play, we realized that she was an accomplished pianist. As it turned out, John was a singer. Together they would lead worship—Angela on piano and John singing. Then John told me about the day Parkinson's hit. They were leading worship together when all of a sudden Angela stopped playing. She couldn't remember the cords. Humiliated, she ran from the building and hadn't touched the piano since. Within a week she was diagnosed with Parkinson's.

As Angela sat on the stage at the keyboard that day of her healing, she began to sing. I will never forget how she sang, "He touched me. Oh, He touched me, and oh, the joy that floods my soul. For something happened and now I know, He touched me and made me whole." It was a glorious moment. There wasn't a dry eye in the church that night.

I am so glad I didn't turn this principle of faith into a law. If I had, I would not have believed that Angela could have been healed. I started out with such small faith, but in each situation God met me right where I was. With Angela I did not have faith at all. In fact, I just felt frustrated that she was asking me to pray for her, when I had clearly said that my emphasis that night would be impartation not healing. In spite of me, God came and healed her anyway.

#2: SIN BLOCKS HEALING

For many people in healing ministry the "go-to" response when someone is not experiencing healing is to think that sin is blocking the healing. Even though sin is a valid reason why people may not be experiencing breakthrough in healing, we cannot assume that everybody who is not receiving healing is dealing with sin. That being said, sin remains a legitimate hindrance to healing.

In Mark 2, we read about the paralyzed man whose four friends brought him to Jesus. Since they could not press through the crowd, they climbed up to the roof, broke through the ceiling, and lowered their paralyzed friend down where Jesus was teaching. Jesus, seeing the man, said, *"Son, your sins are forgiven you"* (Mark 2:5).

The Pharisees got upset because only God could forgive sins, and for Jesus to make a statement absolving this man of sin was, in effect, declaring Himself to be God. They thought such a statement was blasphemy, which it was— unless, of course, it was true. Jesus looked at them and said,

"Why do you reason about these things in your hearts? Which is easier, to say to the paralytic, 'Your sins are forgiven you,' or to say, 'Arise, take up your bed and walk'? But that you may know that the Son of Man has power on earth to forgive sins"—He said to the paralytic, *"I say to you, arise, take up your bed, and go to your house"* (Mark 2:8-11).

That is exactly what happened. We see that *"immediately he arose, took up the bed, and went out in the presence of them all, so that all were amazed and glorified God"* (Mark 2:12).

What was the first thing Jesus said to this paralyzed man? *"Son, your sins are forgiven."* Some diseases and sicknesses are actually related to sin. The key word here is "some." This is not all encompassing for all matters of sickness and disease. Also, you should never allow someone's sin or sinful lifestyle to prevent you from praying for healing. You might need to help them identify areas that need forgiveness, repentance, inner healing, or confession of sin. However, trust the Holy Spirit to bring this up during the interview process. Do not push it. Simply wait on the Lord and follow His direction, especially if you find yourself dealing with sensitive matters of sin.

There are some believers who take the principle that sin blocks healing too far. Some churches actually teach that if you are not a Christian, you cannot be healed. This is certainly not true, as healing is an evangelistic sign and wonder that has historically ushered unsaved people into the Kingdom of God. Some missionaries in India, for example, have taught others not to lay hands on and pray for a Hindu, a Sikh, or a Muslim unless he or she accepts Jesus first. I don't believe this either, as the Lord is renowned for reaching out to these long before they make some kind of profession of faith. We hear about Muslims having visions and dreams of the "man in white," who has been leading many of them to faith in Christ. God reaches out to them supernaturally. That act, be it a vision, dream, or miraculous healing, serves as a catalyst to demonstrate the reliability of the gospel and the supremacy of Jesus Christ.

YOU SHOULD NEVER ALLOW SOMEONE'S
SIN OR SINFUL LIFESTYLE TO PREVENT
YOU FROM PRAYING FOR HEALING.

Yet some people insist that a person must be saved, clean, and sanctified before we pray for his or her healing. Why? Because they believe that sin in your life can block the flow of healing. This is sometimes true, particularly if a person is backslidden or living in rebellion towards God. At the same time, I have watched God turn this principle on its head in some unusual, miraculous ways.

Woman with a Brain Tumor

Once, when I was involved in relief work through our local food bank, I visited the home of a woman to deliver food. This woman did not know I was a pastor. I just wore a "Feed My People" badge as a volunteer. Our purpose was to go to the lost. We were only assigned to go to homes that had indicated no church affiliation.

The woman at this particular house was about twenty-five. She was not saved, had been living with a man, and had two children out of wedlock, ages five and seven. The man she had been living with left her after emptying her bank account and stealing her car. She was totally destitute. On top of that she had terminal cancer—an inoperable brain tumor. She had tried chemo, but it had not worked. The doctor told her, "Make your will out; you are going to die."

She was born into a Lutheran family, was baptized as a baby, and had gone to church once since then. The only prayer she knew was, "Now I lay me down to sleep," and she only knew that one line. This woman had no experience with the church at all. I didn't tell her I was a pastor, I just said, "I believe that God still heals today. Can I pray for you? I have seen people get healed when I pray for them."

She agreed to let me pray for her and so I began to pray, right there. It surprised her. She wasn't used to people praying right then and there. Her experience was to have people ask if they could pray for her and then they would go home and pray, rather than praying on the spot. She was surprised and not very comfortable with the idea of me praying right then and there. I said to her, "God can heal you from a distance, but that's akin to graduate level healing. I am still in remedial school, and I just do not have enough faith for that. I am being honest with you. The likelihood of healing happening through my prayers from a distance is not nearly as strong as if you will let me pray for you right here and right now. I have faith for that."

She agreed to let me pray right there, but she wouldn't close her eyes when I asked. Understand, there is nothing holy about closing your eyes; I just get nervous when someone is looking directly at me while I'm praying for them. I moved over to the side so that I would not be looking her in the eye, and I started praying for her. A couple of the women who were with our food distribution team were also there praying for her.

"My head is getting hot," she said. "That's good!" I replied. "You are weird," was her response. I just ignored that and kept praying. Then she said, "I feel electricity all over my head." "That's *really* good," I replied. And she said, "You're *really* weird."

As we prayed, she kept talking—and she wouldn't stop! Truly, this woman was not "church broken" yet. In fact, I was thinking, "Gosh! She needs to be quiet so that the Spirit can work on her. She needs to focus on what she is receiving so she can recognize it," but she just kept talking. Then I felt like the Holy Spirit said, "Don't worry about it; this one is on Me. Nothing that she does is going to stop her healing from happening." We just kept praying, and then we left.

Every two weeks we took more food over to her and prayed for her brain tumor. Every time, on four separate occasions, she felt heat and electricity in her body. Finally, another man moved in, so she called the food bank and told them to stop coming because she didn't need help anymore.

I didn't know what happened to her until several years later. I was at the food bank again and I saw her. "You're still alive!" I shouted across the room. She ran over to shush me but I was so excited that I insisted she tell me what had happened. After our prayer sessions she had returned to the doctor for another MRI. The brain tumor had metastasized to her breast and abdomen, or so they thought. When they did the MRI, they couldn't find one tumor anywhere except for an empty spot in her head where the tumor used to be.

Then she said, "You know, I always wondered if it had anything to do with you guys praying for me." I told her more about healing prayer. The next part of the story really blows me away. I said to her, "It was the Lord who healed you. I am training a new ministry team at my church to do what we do. Would you be willing to come and share your story?"

I was talking to an unsaved woman who was living with a guy she wasn't married to, and she said, "Yes. I would be glad to come to your church and tell the people what He did for me." Now something is wrong with this picture when an unbelieving woman living with a man is more willing to tell her testimony than people who are in the church and are Christians. People get saved, and yet they will not tell their testimonies. We need to share our testimonies because it is not about us; it is about Jesus. We are all trophies of His grace.

This woman came to our ministry team training and started to give her testimony. When she got to the part about making her will for her five-and seven-year-old daughters, she broke down and started crying. At that moment she was not very far from the Kingdom, and I trust that by now the Lord has brought her all the way into the Kingdom. But if I had thought that sin could stop a healing I would never have had the faith for this unsaved woman to be healed.

But do you know what? I have the greatest faith and the greatest expectation for healing to take place when I go to the poor and to the lost. I know healing is a powerful tool for evangelism.

#3: THE PRINCIPLE OF THE ANOINTED PERSON

When I was really young, and still a Baptist pastor, I was desperate to see a breakthrough in healing. The only healing I knew of was my own healing from severe injuries received in a car accident.

Woman with Amputated Leg and Severe Pain

Pressing in at that point in my life and ministry, I thought that a hospital would be a good place to possibly see healing. I located one in a nearby coal mining community and was there in the hospital praying for a man when I heard a woman across the hall, moaning in pain. I went over, knocked on her door, and she invited me in. I said, "Hi. My name is Randy Clark, and I'm a Baptist pastor. I heard you moaning and I know you are in pain. I believe that God can heal and I want to pray for you. Can I pray for you?"

Her response took me off-guard. She said, "No! You can't. I don't believe that it would do any good." Hoping to continue to engage her, I responded, "Well, you may be right and probably are, but you don't have anything to lose."

The woman shared her story with me. She was a coal miner and the roof had caved in on her, amputating her leg. She had also suffered a spinal injury that left her in severe pain. It was very obvious that this woman was suffering a great deal. She said to me, "Listen! I believed that if I got to Tulsa to a camp meeting and had Brother Kenneth Hagin pray for me, I would be healed. So I went, and he prayed for me and I wasn't healed. And if I wasn't healed when Brother Hagin prayed for me, I am not about to be healed when you pray for me."

Let's stop right there for a moment. The principle of the anointed person *is* certainly a valid principle since there have been anointed people like Kenneth Hagin, Kathryn Kuhlman, Oral Roberts, and other healing evangelists with powerful ministries of healing. I honor these individuals. This story is not meant in any way to disparage Hagin because he really did have a powerful ministry of healing. Every healing evangelist has experienced the agony of defeat. Just because someone is not healed under a certain person's ministry does not give us the right to denounce the healing evangelist as false or phony. We are all simply human. These evangelists have to navigate through the agony of defeat in the same way you and I do. This woman specifically viewed Kenneth Hagin as an anointed individual, and assumed that if she was not healed at his camp meeting, there was really no hope for her. This is where we discover the very surprising nature of our God and how He delights to anoint anyone at anytime.

I said to the woman, "You don't have anything to lose. Just let me pray for you." She finally agreed and so and I prayed for her and her headaches and severe pain left! This shocked the both of us because there was hardly any faith in the room. In addition, I did not consider myself to be an anointed person. My track record was nonexistent, since this was one of the first healings I ever saw in my life. Yes, there are people who truly have the gift of healing, but I want to remind you that everybody can be used for healing in Jesus' name. That is the whole purpose of this book. The power to heal lives on the inside of us in the person of the Holy Spirit. This is the well of power we draw from when praying for the sick, and it is truly where I had to go when I prayed for this coal miner.

"MORE PEOPLE GET HEALED WHEN
MORE PEOPLE PRAY FOR HEALING."

If I had turned the principle of the anointed person into a law, I would have immediately left her room without praying for her. But I have never believed that God could only use these "men and women of power for the hour." I have always believed that all Christians have been graciously invited into the ministry of healing. We are all commissioned to pray for the sick. As one of my friends has said, the essence of my message can be summed up in one sentence: "More people get healed when more people pray for healing."

An Unchurched Woman with Crohn's Disease

I was ministering in England once, at a meeting of about a thousand people, and I was praying for the sick. There was a woman there who had heard me share the testimony of someone healed of Crohn's disease after receiving prayer. This woman's unbelieving sister had the same condition. As I shared this testimony the believing sister felt heat coming into her abdominal area, fell out of her seat, and went to call her mother. She said, "We have to get my sister to come to church. I believe that God will heal her if she will come."

So they called the unbelieving sister, and the first miracle that took place was that she actually came to church. We had a team there, who were all praying for the sick. Somehow, when I came over to the sister with Crohn's disease, I accidentally skipped over her. I didn't do it on purpose. I didn't even know I had done it. I would not know it until this day had they not written me a letter.

The believing sister wrote to me later on explaining what happened. At first, she had wanted to call over to me and say, "Randy, come back here! You have got to pray for my sister!" However, the Holy Spirit told her, "Don't look to the man, look to Me." So she didn't call for me to come back, and I continued on, praying for other people. The believing sister recounts how she began to pray, "God, if it is not Randy, bring the senior pastor, Wes Richards; and if it is not Wes, bring one of the associate pastors; and if it is not him, bring at least one of the elders." She was looking for an anointed man or woman to pray for her sister with Crohn's.

GOD WILL OFTEN PERFORM THE GREATEST
MIRACLES THROUGH SOMEONE WHO IS STEPPING
OUT FOR THE FIRST TIME TO PRAY FOR THE SICK.

Who stepped up and offered to pray? The youngest person on our ministry team—a girl of about thirteen or fifteen—skipped up to her and asked, "Can I pray for you?" Her first reaction was, "Oh, no God! Not a teenage girl—at least an elder!" This teenage girl did not fit the mold of what the anointed vessel of power should look like. The little girl put her hand on the woman's abdominal area and as she began to pray, the unbelieving woman was healed of incurable Crohn's disease. Within just a few weeks, this woman was back at work, and I received a letter from her sister eight months later confirming the healing. The important point to remember is this: there are anointed people, but God will often perform the greatest miracles through someone who is stepping out for the first time to pray for the sick.

#4: THE PRINCIPLE OF FEELING THE ANOINTING

There is a principle called "feeling the anointing," and we see it beautifully illustrated in a story from the gospel of Mark. *"Immediately the fountain of her blood was dried up, and she felt in her body that she was healed of the affliction. And Jesus, immediately knowing in Himself that power had gone out of Him, turned around in the crowd and said, "Who touched My clothes?"* (Mark 5:29-30).

In verse 33 we read that the woman came forward and fell at Jesus' feet, trembling with fear as she confessed that she had touched the hem of his garment. I personally think she was trembling with fear because she was caught. *"But His disciples said to Him, "You see the multitude thronging You, and You say, 'Who touched Me'" And He looked around to see her who had done this thing. But the woman, fearing and trembling, knowing what had happened to her, came and fell down before Him and told Him the whole truth"* (Mark 5:31-33). The Scripture explains that He felt virtue or power come out of Him, and it went into her (see Mark 5:30). Jesus knew that something was released out of Him because of her faith.

There are times as you are praying for the sick when you can physically feel the anointing—the presence of God—flowing out of you. Healing evangelists William Branham and Oral Roberts claimed to feel the anointing in their hands as they ministered to the sick.

Anointing for a Missionary

Once I prayed for a man who was preparing to be a missionary (I didn't know this at the time). All I knew was that there were a lot of people to pray for, and I had to move quickly down the line. He came up for prayer, and I said, "Put your hand out." I just touched his hand and said, "I bless you," and I walked on.

I didn't know he had driven several hours to get there—that he was hoping to receive more than just that simple prayer. I didn't know he was headed for a Muslim country as a missionary. But what I didn't know, God knew. If I had known those things, I would have certainly spent more time with him. Anyway, I moved on, and he was mad at me. But all of a sudden, he realized, "Well, wait a minute, I feel burning in my hands." The burning sensation just kept growing until the whole palm of his hand was hot.

He went off to do his missionary work with an evangelical group, and the mission failed, so they closed it down, but by faith he stayed. Every time the palm of his hand got hot, he knew God wanted to heal someone. He would extend an invitation to pray by saying "Who is sick?" He was physically feeling the anointing.

This phenomenon doesn't happen to me, although I think it would be quite an advantage. What if you don't feel the anointing? Does this make you less spiritual or qualified for healing ministry? Absolutely not. Remember, do not make a law out of the principle. God does allow some people to "feel the anointing" by giving them a physical sensation in their body, but this doesn't happen to everyone. Whether or not you can feel the anointing, pray and let God move as He wills. Just keep praying and doing what the Spirit instructs you to do.

#5: THE PRINCIPLE OF MOVING WITH COMPASSION

In Matthew 14:14, and in other places throughout the gospels, Scripture shows us how Jesus was moved by compassion, as He healed the sick. If faith is the greatest principle of all, then compassion is the second greatest principle. Allow yourself to be moved with compassion—follow your heart.

Many of the healings I have seen come about when God tugs at my heart. I don't know why, but when I begin to talk to somebody and find out that they have this problem or that condition, I find myself wanting to pray for them. This is just the way the Spirit has led me, and I believe it is the compassion of God moving in my heart.

In the Dungeon

I was in Minneapolis/St. Paul for the first time, about six months after the renewal began in Toronto. At that point, I had hardly ever traveled, but I was nearing the end of thirty days of travel in a row. I was exhausted, and this was the last meeting before I was to go home. I missed my wife and my four children who were one, three, eight, and twelve at the time. On top of it all, I was staying in the home of someone from the church—in the unfinished basement of a small house. It had a commode that didn't work right to begin with and sprayed water everywhere when I broke it. My associate and I had to get towels to sop up the water. It was a dark, dingy, yucky place.

I was discouraged to say the least. Besides that, the meeting was one of the weirdest meetings we had that year. We had about two thousand people in this big old building we had rented. There were two people involved in the occult who were dressed in black with black stuff all over them. One woman would run into the crowd with a large cupful of water and dump it over somebody's head, then run away while the people in charge tried to catch her. Another guy would go up to any empty microphone and start cussing. There was some unusual warfare going on to say the least.

As I reached the end of my message, I gave the invitation: "How many of you want to receive the Father's blessing?" This invitation always brings a lot of joy and, at that particular meeting, a lot of people were getting "drunk" in the Spirit as they received. About 1,500 people, or three-quarters of the audience responded to the invitation and were directed to one area of the room.

At this time in my ministry the Spirit was moving with such power that those I trained for ministry had only to walk by someone and say, "Fill!" and the person would go out in the power of the Spirit. Those were exciting times and it was fun to minister. About 75 of my trained ministers headed for the group who wanted to receive the Father's blessing.

Then I gave another invitation: "How many of you are sick and need to be healed?" About five hundred people headed over to the healing area with twenty-five of my healing team. I thought, "Oh God, I want to go over there with the Father's blessing group, where the fun is, not with the sick people." This is when I sensed that Jesus would rather have me with the sick. His compassion always directed Him towards the sick, afflicted, and tormented.

I went over to the group of sick people. I knew in my spirit that's where I was supposed to be, but in my flesh I didn't want to be there. When the first person came up, I crossed my arms and said, "So what's wrong with you?" It was more of an accusation than a question! Then I prayed and nothing happened. Another person came. I asked the same question. I prayed again, and nothing. This went on for a while.

Man with Hurting Toes

Then I got to this big guy: he was about six foot six, maybe 275 pounds, and roughly seventy-five years old. I asked, "What's wrong with you?" and he replied, "My big toe hurts." My body language must have said something negative because immediately he looked at me and he said, "No! No! My big toe really does hurt, and it is hard to minister when your toes are hurting."

Reluctantly, I told him to take off his shoes and socks. I got down on my knees and took a big toe in each hand. I am a farm boy, and the only thing I could think of was the motion of milking a cow. Here I was in Minneapolis/ St. Paul, in front of 2,000 people talking to this guy's toes, because I teach that we are to speak to the condition when we pray. So I was talking to his toes saying things like, "Big toe, stop hurting! I command you in Jesus' name! Toes, stop hurting! I command the pain in these toes to leave! Toes, I tell you: stop hurting!"

Then I got this impression from the devil: "Are you aware of how stupid you look right now?" I *was* aware and hoping nobody would notice. I had prayed for five people, and none of them had been healed. Five down and 495 to go! At that moment I was overwhelmed with depression, despair, and discouragement. I thought, "God, I don't want to do this anymore. I just want to quit." Thankfully I didn't say that out loud.

Realizing I was in trouble, I knew it was time for "the secret preacher prayer." The secret preacher prayer is the kind of prayer a preacher prays that is so brutally honest that it has to be prayed in secret, because if anyone else heard it, it would suck all the faith out of the room. I went into secret preacher prayer mode, and underneath my breath I started praying, "Lord, the Bible says that we're to co-labor with You. I'm here, where are *You*? Nothing is happening. I don't want to do this anymore, Lord. This is not working. I want to go back to the basement and put the covers over my head until I can go home tomorrow."

Right then and there, the Lord took me into one of the few visions I have ever had in my entire life. In the vision, I saw myself at seven years of age, when I was kicked in the head by a horse and was nearly killed. You could see the hoof print in my head and see my skull. I was a half-mile away from home, and I had to run there with blood streaming down my face. My dad took me to the doctor, who said if the hoof had been a quarter of an inch closer, or I had turned my head, I would have been dead.

Can you imagine how fearful I was of horses after that? It wasn't until I was twelve that I started to ride again. I remember my dad said to me, "Son, if that horse throws you, you must get up and get back on it and ride it, or you will never ride again. Fear will take over." Then the vision ended.

I knew exactly how to interpret this picture and I knew precisely what it meant. God used the natural to explain the spiritual to me. He was saying, "You've been thrown off with guilt and shame, and all of this stuff is coming against you.

If you stop now and go back to that dingy basement and hide, you may never pray for the sick again."

I had no doubt that this vision was from God. Immediately, I started to encourage myself in the Lord. I knew He had heard my prayer. I came out of secret preacher prayer mode and went back to normal prayer mode. "Big toes," I said. "In the name of Jesus, I command you to stop hurting!" I prayed for that man's toes and we prayed for all five hundred people that night, and many of them were healed.

Woman with Lung Cancer

Afterwards, as I went to sit down, a woman came over and asked if she could pray for me. I told her that she could, and as she began to pray, I felt electricity go through my entire body. I felt the anointing and presence of God. I hadn't felt it the whole time I was praying for the sick, but when this woman prayed, I felt saturated in God's presence. He was refreshing me and it was absolutely wonderful.

When she had finished praying for me, she asked if I would pray for her. I just assumed she wanted an impartation, but that was not the case. She was dying of cancer and wanted prayer for healing. She had twenty-eight tumors in her lungs, tumors in her neck and in her lymph nodes. Within seconds of starting to pray for her, she began to feel burning in her lungs as God began to heal her. God was there, collaborating with me to release His power. I am so glad I didn't give up that night. I could have listened to Satan's mocking voice and run back to that damp basement to hide, but instead I choose to stay and pray, and God showed up.

THAT'S WHEN IT'S TIME FOR SOMEBODY TO PUT A LITTLE LOVE IN YOU SO THAT YOU CAN KEEP ON GIVING LOVE AWAY.

Overcoming Compassion Fatigue

I didn't know it at the time, but I was suffering from compassion fatigue. I felt no compassion for the people in need of healing. All I felt was overwhelming exhaustion. If you are a parent you understand compassion fatigue. Every parent reaches that point with their children from time to time. That's when it's time for somebody to put a little love in you so that you can keep on giving love away. Compassion fatigue makes you feel depleted and empty. It's not that you have stopped loving your children. You are just running on empty. Mothers get it and so do nurses and teachers and ministers, to name a few.

When we are suffering from compassion fatigue, the enemy will try to exploit it. He comes in, twists the Bible, and says things like, "Jesus moved with compassion to heal the sick." Immediately you feel guilty because your compassion does not measure up to Jesus' compassion. Next, the devil tries to convince you that because you don't have any compassion, you are not qualified to minister healing. He tries to use the principle of compassion *against* you, thereby disqualifying you from praying for the sick. If you believe his lies, they will suck all the faith right out of you. If you believe your compassion fatigue disqualifies you from operating in

God's healing power, you will most likely not pray for the sick, and that's just what Satan wants.

IF YOU BELIEVE YOUR COMPASSION FATIGUE
DISQUALIFIES YOU FROM OPERATING IN
GOD'S HEALING POWER, YOU WILL MOST
LIKELY NOT PRAY FOR THE SICK.

Faith in Jesus

We have examined five important principles that apply to the ministry of healing.

As you pray for healing, you don't have to meet every condition listed in this chapter. When I pray for the sick, my faith isn't in my performance. My faith is in Jesus and what He did on the cross. When I don't feel anything, when I am in a bad mood and the devil starts beating me up, I just get on my knees, and I pray: "Lord, I know I haven't measured up, but it is not about me, it is about You. And Lord, I am asking You to loose Your healing anointing for the sake of the people. Do not let my shortcomings keep You from moving and touching the people. I have so much faith in God's love for people, that even when I feel unqualified or underserving, I can press in and pray for healing, because I know it is God who heals, not me. He uses us because He loves *them*.

NOTE

1. I would say that 80 percent of the greatest miracles that we have seen actually happen in the last thirty minutes before we leave. Sometimes, it's the very last person we pray for.

PART 6

WORDS OF KNOWLEDGE

Chapter 18

WORDS OF KNOWLEDGE
FOR HEALING

UNLOCK GOD'S PROPHETIC POWER

The story of blind Bartimeaus in the Gospel of Mark is a powerful illustration of how the word of knowledge works. Consider the story and its implications for how the Holy Spirit wants to equip you to minister healing:

> *Now they came to Jericho. As He went out of Jericho with His disciples and a great multitude, blind Barti-maeus, the son of Timaeus, sat by the road begging. And when he heard that it was Jesus of Nazareth, he began to cry out and say, "Jesus, Son of David, have mercy on me!"* (Mark 10:46-47).

Blind Bartimaeus' cries exemplify the cries of the sick and needy that we are commissioned to respond to. There are many people like Bartimaeus, who are suffering. As Christians who are filled with and empowered by the Spirit, we can be the catalyst for divine healing to these people. Let's look more closely at the story.

MY PRAYER IS THAT THE BODY OF CHRIST WOULD BECOME SUCH A STRONG FORCE FOR HEALING IN THE WORLD THAT THE PEOPLE AROUND US WOULD TAKE NOTICE.

As Jesus and His disciples went out of Jericho, followed by the great multitude, there was a beggar named Bartimaeus who sat alongside the road. When Bartimaeus heard that it was Jesus who was passing by, he began to cry out for mercy. He was aware of who Jesus represented and what He carried. Are the people around you aware of who you represent and what you carry? We are ambassadors of the living God, jars of clay (2 Cor. 4:7), filled with the Spirit of God who alone has the power to heal sickness and destroy the works of the devil. My prayer is that the body of Christ would become such a strong force for healing in the world that the people around us would take notice.

Bartimaeus knew Jesus had something that, in a moment, could change his life forever. He had nothing to lose, so he cried out. *"Then many warned him to be quiet; but he cried out all the more, "Son of David, have mercy on me!" So Jesus stood still and commanded him to be called. Then they called the blind man, saying to him, "Be of good cheer. Rise, He is calling you"* (Mark 10:48-49).

Here we see a powerful illustration of the word of knowledge in action. The text tells us that Jesus *stood still*. Jesus did not walk over to Bartimaeus. Instead, He instructed His followers to call the blind man to Him. When you receive a word of knowledge for healing, it is as if Jesus is using you to tell someone else, "Be encouraged! Get up and come. Jesus is calling you!" When you receive divine insight into someone's specific condition, call it out!

When a person responds to a word of knowledge, many things begin to take place, not the least of which is that they are being brought to Jesus. Healing is wonderful and we desire that for everyone, but there is nothing more glorious than to see someone come into the arms of Jesus. In the pages ahead, as you study the word of knowledge, I encourage you not to turn it into some kind of religious principle or law. The word of knowledge should be normative, but not "common." It should be a normal part of our lives as we pray for the sick, but at the same time we should never see words of knowledge as a common thing. Every word you receive and deliver reveals God's heart to heal and to draw people closer to Him.

MY HISTORY WITH WORDS OF KNOWLEDGE

I was actually in ministry fourteen years before I recognized how to receive a word of knowledge. I had a degree in religious studies and a master of divinity, yet no practical understanding of how to move in this gift of the Holy Spirit. The very week I was given a few brief instruction about words of knowledge, I began to operate in this gift.

Most of us simply need teaching about the gifts of the Spirit in order to give us confidence to step out and activate them in our lives. One week after I began receiving words of knowledge, I taught on the subject for the first time. That same evening, a woman received a word that led to a healing. Every time I have taught on this subject since then, and have given God the opportunity to move, people have received their first word of knowledge. I have taught about words of knowledge hundreds of times, and now I pray that these practical instructions help you begin to hear from God in a powerful new way.

MOST OF US SIMPLY NEED TEACHING
ABOUT THE GIFTS OF THE SPIRIT IN ORDER
TO GIVE US CONFIDENCE TO STEP OUT
AND ACTIVATE THEM IN OUR LIVES.

THE WORD OF KNOWLEDGE

There are diversities of gifts, but the same Spirit. There are differences of ministries, but the same Lord. And there are diversities of activities, but it is the same God who works all in all. But the manifestation of the Spirit is given to each one for the profit of all: for to one is given the word of wisdom through the Spirit, to another the word of knowledge through the same Spirit... (1 Corinthians 12:4-8).

When you receive a word of knowledge, it is for the purpose of releasing the love and power of Jesus to someone else.

But just what is a word of knowledge? It is a supernatural revelation of information given by the Holy Spirit, knowledge received apart from natural analysis or human means. Paul actually received many of his revelations through words of knowledge. He writes: *"Now we have received, not the spirit of the world, but the Spirit who is from God, that we might know the things that have been freely given to us by God. These things we also speak, not in words which man's wisdom teaches but which the Holy Spirit teaches..."* (1 Corinthians 2:12-13).

IT IS A SUPERNATURAL REVELATION OF INFORMATION GIVEN BY THE HOLY SPIRIT.

WORDS OF KNOWLEDGE FOR HEALING

The Holy Spirit will often give a revelatory word of knowledge concerning the needs of a person (or multiple people) for healing. This is an indication that God wishes to heal the person or those who have the condition revealed through the word of knowledge, and it is often an indication that God wishes to heal at the time the word is given. When understood in this way, a word of knowledge does two things. First, it builds faith in the person who needs the healing, and second, it strengthens the faith of the person who shared the word of knowledge.

Consider the following example: You receive a word of knowledge that Dan is suffering from painful migraine headaches with nausea. Maybe you run into Dan at the grocery store or your desk is positioned next to his at work. The Holy Spirit might simply say something to you like "migraines and nausea" when you look at Dan. When you share that with him (and he has never told you about his migraines or expressed that he suffers from any of these conditions), that word releases faith. Dan might think to himself, "Wow, this person just called out my condition without any knowledge of what I have been going through."

THE HOLY SPIRIT FREQUENTLY USES WORDS OF KNOWLEDGE EVANGELISTICALLY, MINISTERING TO THOSE WHO DO NOT KNOW JESUS.

Whether Dan is a Christian or not, faith has been released through that word. If Dan is a believer, then his faith will be strengthened to believe that God desires to heal him. If Dan is not a Christian, the hope is that this word of knowledge for healing will plant a seed in his heart to ultimately respond to the gospel. You will find that the Holy Spirit frequently uses words of knowledge evangelistically, ministering to those who do not know Jesus.

Words of knowledge reveal God's undeniable supernatural nature since they come from a supernatural source. They also expresses His compassionate and loving nature, in the same way they did when Jesus called blind Bartimaeus to come.

In addition, as you share a word of knowledge with someone and the person confirms that the word is in fact accurate, your personal faith level rises. You become increasingly confident to minister in words of knowledge—to take risks, responding to the Holy Spirit's promptings.

Once you receive a word of knowledge, you should speak it out at that very moment, or at the next appropriate time. Once you share the word, see if it applies to anyone present. If so, offer to pray for them at once for healing—whether the word applies to an individual or to a group.

SPECIFICITY IN WORDS OF KNOWLEDGE FOR HEALING

The more specific the word of knowledge, the more faith it will build in the people involved. If you receive the word by feeling a pain, it is helpful for you to identify the kind of pain and specify its exact location in the body. For example: It is better to say, "A shooting pain on the left side of the neck just below the ear," or to point to the exact location, than to merely state, "A pain in the neck," or ask, "Does someone's neck hurt?" Instead of simply saying, "back pain," say, "Pain in the third lumbar vertebra," or to point to the exact location that has been revealed to you by the Holy Spirit.

When you receive a word of knowledge, be careful not to change it or add to it. You should not exaggerate the word, nor should you leave out a detail that seems unimportant to you. Everything is intentional and has meaning, while changes or additions cause confusion. For example: a person received a mental picture of someone being injured by tripping over a green hose. The only green hoses he had seen were garden hoses. So he said he had a picture of a person injured by tripping over a green *garden* hose. There was a man in the meeting who had been injured by tripping over a green *pressure* hose at work. He did not respond to the word at first, because the hose he tripped over was not a *garden* hose. He would have responded more quickly to the word of knowledge if the person receiving the revelation had not added to it.

Maintain the integrity and purity of the word you receive. Even the smallest detail can release significant faith to the person listening. When we manipulate or adjust the word, we run the risk of causing people not to respond. If they hear something in the word that sounds partially correct, but they also hear the stuff we decided to add in, there is a strong possibility that their confusion will keep them from responding. We must stick to the word we have been given!

Chapter 19

GIVING WORDS OF KNOWLEDGE

You may receive a word of knowledge anywhere and at any time. You might get a word during a prayer meeting, a small group meeting, walking past someone in church or in the supermarket, or while washing dishes at home. You may or may not know for whom the revelation has been given.

Most often than not, the word of knowledge is given for someone who is present. If you are in church and you receive the word, most likely it is for someone in the church. Likewise, if you get a word of knowledge in the checkout line at the supermarket, it is probably applicable to someone standing near you.

There is also the chance that the word may be for someone who is not present, but is intended for someone they know, such as the sister of the cashier who is checking your groceries. Or the word could be for somebody you will see tomorrow or next week. When in doubt, ask the Holy Spirit for direction.

HOW DOES GOD GIVE WORDS OF KNOWLEDGE FOR HEALING?

God gives His revelation in different ways. This is true of words of knowledge for healing as well as for other kinds of revelation. My early education about words of knowledge came during a telephone call with Vineyard leader, Lance Pittluck. Lance had interviewed many people who operated in words of knowledge. Based on his observations and research, he concluded that there are approximately six common ways people receive words of knowledge for healing.

The first way is through feeling. You may feel a certain condition or sensation in your body such as a sharp pain, a throbbing sensation, or a strong emotion, such as fear or panic. Be careful that your feeling is not caused by a condition in your own body. For instance, if you often have pain in your left ear, you would not share that as a word of knowledge, even if you get that pain during a meeting.

A second way to receive a word of knowledge is to "see" it. When a word comes out of the blue, you might receive a picture in your mind that reveals a condition. These pictures can look something like a body part—perhaps a heart, a foot, an eye, or a head—or a person with a certain condition, such as a limp; a person carefully holding his arm; or a crutch, eyeglasses, or a person walking with a cane. You might even see things like an auto accident or the scene of an injury.

When it comes to images, visions, and mental pictures, be careful not to assume an interpretation. I will never forget one instance where someone got the phrase "water bottle." That is all they received, and in obedience to the Holy Spirit, they called out "water bottle." They did not provide any kind of "prophetic" interpretation or specification; they just said "water bottle" and trusted God to use it however He wanted. Amazingly, that unique word of knowledge delivered in that specific format was exactly what a person in the audience needed to receive healing.

A third way to receive a word of knowledge is to "read" it. You may see the condition in your mind or actually see the condition's name written over the person you are receiving the word for. This might look like a person with a word written across their front or back or over their head, or on their forehead. Sometimes people see a word written on a wall or on the carpet, or see something like a newspaper headline, or a banner.

You can also receive words of knowledge as an impression. You may sense in your mind (a mental impression) that someone has a particular condition. Or you may sense the Holy Spirit speaking to you, which comes to you like a thought popping into your mind.

Sometimes you may suddenly and unexpectedly speak out a word of knowledge. You may be talking, or praying with someone, and unplanned words suddenly tumble out of your mouth relating to something you were not aware of.

Words of knowledge can also come through a dream or a vision. You may have a vivid dream or a vision in which you have a new health problem, or you see someone else with a health problem, or you hear someone talking about a health problem.

There is an arbitrary nature to the ways in which words of knowledge come to us. Most often, when a word comes out of the blue, you will know that the Holy Spirit is communicating something to you. There will typically be no rhyme or reason for the pain or condition you experience. Just be sure to evaluate whether it is pain you are personally experiencing in your own body, or it is a spiritual sensitivity to what God wants to do in that context.

HOW TO SPEAK WHEN YOU BELIEVE YOU HAVE RECEIVED A WORD OF KNOWLEDGE

It is generally wise, at least in the beginning, to be tentative about speaking out a word of knowledge you receive. Exercise humility. If you have never received a word of knowledge before, I encourage you to practice in a safe environment, exercising balance and sensitivity to the Holy Spirit. Even though we are called to be confident in Christ, there is an appropriate caution to maintain, especially when you are starting out. Learn to discern what is of you and what the Holy Spirit reveals. This is a process, and it requires practice. Be encouraged because with practice comes failure and lots of it. Do not deliver a word with 100 percent confidence when, in fact, you are uncertain. Be real and authentic. Don't try to put on a mask.

In the same way that not everyone receives healing, not every word of knowledge you share will be received. Over time, you will surely see an increase, both in your level of accuracy in receiving from God, your specificity in delivering the word, and also the number of people who respond to the words.

If you are part of a small group, practice when you meet. If you feel you have received a word of knowledge for someone start out by saying something like, "Does anyone have a sharp pain in their left elbow just now?" If no one responds, don't be concerned or embarrassed. Let's say that Sarah responds, confirming that the word applies to her. You could say, "Well, I just had a sharp pain in my left elbow, which may be a word of knowledge indicating that God would like to heal you now, since you have that condition. Would you like for me (or us) to pray for you now?"

If Sarah is open to receiving prayer, pray for her. If she wants prayer later, pray for her later. If she doesn't want prayer due to embarrassment, lovingly encourage her to receive. If she still refuses, don't pressure her in any way to receive prayer. Healing is one fruit of sharing a word of knowledge; the other fruits should be love and compassion. While we should encourage people to receive prayer, we do not want to force or pressure anyone.

If you believe you have received a word of knowledge for healing in a larger meeting or church service, you should probably not speak out unless there is an appropriate moment indicated by the leader or pastor. The opportunity may not come during the service, however, I would encourage you to "keep your antennae up" to see whether God puts someone in your path later on who has the condition revealed to you. Even though I recommended praying immediately after receiving a word of knowledge, this is not by any means a law. If you receive a word of knowledge in a larger meeting, ask the Holy Spirit to show you who the word is intended for. You can then deliver it after the service, in a more appropriate setting.

PRACTICAL TOOLS TO HELP YOU GROW IN WORDS OF KNOWLEDGE FOR HEALING

Here are some guidelines to consider as you receive and share words of knowledge for healing. Let's begin with the *"speed of receiving."* A word of knowledge for healing may come quickly, flitting through your mind more like a bird or dancing butterfly than a stationary billboard. Or it could be a *"first impression."* Either way, once you receive the word, it may seem rather vague. Don't let this tempt you to screen it out and ignore the word. You need to practice "tuning in" to these revelations and begin speaking them out. It takes time to develop your "hearing" muscles when it comes to words of knowledge. Work with whatever you are hearing, pressing in until you are satisfied you are not going to hear anything more or different. Then go with what you have, however unusual it may seem at the moment. If you are tentative and humble, not arrogant or presumptuous, no one will be offended if you seem to have heard incorrectly.

Resist the temptation to believe that a word you received is not important. The details matter. Also, do not be quick to reject perceived words of knowledge, thinking that it is "just you" making up the word. Step out and take the risk. Remember, when you share the word of knowledge, it will build faith in the person receiving it since they will know that God has revealed their conditions to you. What might seem like a vague impression to you may be a shout to the other person!

Don't presume anything. We need to be very careful in the language we use, as it can either keep the conversation going or shut it down entirely. Do not be presumptuous and say something like, "God just told me that you have an earache." If we immediately come out saying, God just told me that you have X condition," and the person does not have that condition, we begin to discredit ourselves. Instead, say something like, "Does your left ear ever bother you?" Or, "I feel like I'm receiving an impression of a problem in a left ear. Does this mean anything to you?" Other examples could include, "Does a picture of a flower vase mean anything to you?" Or, "I think I see a picture of cows in a field. Does that have any significance for you?"

As I mentioned before, it is important to be specific. Be as specific as the word revealed to you. The more specific the word, the more it builds faith in you and in the person or people you are ministering to. Also, be honest. Unpretentious honesty is the best policy when sharing a word of knowledge. It's perfectly okay to admit that you're nervous, say that you have only a vague impression, say that you have never had a word of knowledge before, or say that praying for sick people is new to you. If these things are true, it is okay to admit it.

Lastly, don't be afraid. Do not let fear rob you or the person who might have been healed through your word of knowledge. Someone once said that "faith" is spelled "r-i-s-k." Be patient, but step out. Be humble, but step out. Be tentative, but step out. God will give you words of knowledge because He wants you to use them. He wants you to use them wisely, prudently, and humbly, but He wants you to *use* them.

WORDS OF KNOWLEDGE AS A POWERFUL TOOL FOR EVANGELISM

Many people are familiar with the idea of prayer for healing in the sense that parishioners in church or in a prayer group will pray for healing for someone who is in the hospital or sick at home, but there is little expectation for immediate engagement in healing prayer. And not only do people not expect or want prayer "right then and there," but they do not expect healing to come about as a result of prayer. Typically, the most that is expected is that the sick person might recover more quickly.

Even in instances where recovery is shortened somewhat, this type of experience is not especially impressive to unbelievers. Healing on the spot, however, in the name of Jesus, can have considerably more impact on someone who is not yet a believer. On-the-spot healing can cause people to respond to Jesus who otherwise might never do so. It is a demonstration of the power of God in the name of Jesus. It is a demonstration that Jesus is concerned about people, and about their needs. It is also a demonstration that the name of

Jesus is more powerful than the works of Satan. We see this in the gospels, and the book of Acts. A word of knowledge can bring an unbeliever right into the arms of Jesus.

Words of knowledge also introduce people to the reality of God. When it is clear that you have received supernatural information about a condition—knowledge you could not have received through any natural means—people will pay attention.

GET ACTIVATED

If you have never received a word of knowledge, do not be afraid. God wants you to start operating in this gift. Do not stress or strain, trying to work something up. The gifts of the Spirit are not given to you based on your merit. In fact, the English word for *gift* (in the context of 1 Corinthians 12) comes from the Greek term *charis* or *charisma, which* simply means grace.

Remember, if you desire to be activated in words of knowledge, it's as simple as asking God. Yes, there are things that will help you develop this gift, such as impartation, teaching, and discipleship, but if you want to begin using a gift of the Spirit right now, *all you need to do is ask for it.* The gifts are given to us in the finished work of Jesus Christ—His atonement, and are received when we ask. Gifts are drawn to those who hunger and thirst for spiritual things. And gifts are received through faith, like everything else in the Kingdom of God.

PART 7

FAITH

Chapter 21

FOUR KINDS OF FAITH

I believe there are four basic kinds of faith for healing, and that it is important for you to understand each one if you are to effectively minister God's power to heal. I shared this message on the four levels of faith for the first time when I was in India. As I was getting ready to share it, the Lord gave me a vision, reminding me of a time when I was in Argentina with Omar Cabrera Jr. That night Omar's mother was leading the service. Over and over again, she would say, "I want everybody to stand. I want everybody to pray this prayer with me. Repeat it after me." Then she would say the prayer, and everybody in the whole place would repeat it.

After a while I said, "Omar, I don't understand. Is everybody here a Christian?"

"Oh no!" he said. "We have a lot of lost people here."

"But your mom keeps saying, 'Everybody pray this prayer,'" I responded.

He said, "Yes. That's my mom's theory. She believes if she can get people who don't know Jesus to begin praying to Him about things, then at the end of the service, it will be much easier to get them to pray the prayer of repentance."

The vision ended and I knew immediately what it meant. God was telling me to have the Hindus pray to Jesus for their healing *before* I gave the invitation at the end of the service to accept Him as their Savior. Picture this: gathered together that night were about 100,000 people—the largest crowd I have ever preached to—and this was the message that the Lord had given me!

I began to teach from the four healing stories in the Gospel of Mark, then I would pray with the people twice after each story. We prayed for healing for the specific condition mentioned in the story, and then we prayed for healing for people who had the same level of faith as the person in the story—whether that was a little or a lot.

That night, as I shared these stories with them, you could hear 100,000 people—90 percent of whom were unsaved Hindus—calling on the name of Jesus for healing. About half of them were healed, and then a third of them accepted Jesus as their Savior. I will never forget that night.

We are going to study those four stories I preached in India, but before we get started let me say that the four kinds of faith illustrated in these stories are not unchangeable, timeless laws. They are not binding. I think you will see that in each of the biblical accounts we study, God has both confirmed these expressions of faith and He has moved beyond them. If you consider these stories from the Bible more of a roadmap or blueprint than a fixed formula, you will be able to develop a greater awareness of the different levels of faith demonstrated by the people you pray for, thus giving you the ability to work with unique faith levels.

We will begin by reviewing several different events in the life of Jesus as He ministered to those who were in need of healing. You will find it interesting that Jesus Himself worked with people at different faith levels. This immediately dispels the myth that "you won't get healed if you don't have enough faith." Don't misunderstand me here: faith is very important. I say it time after time—when more faith is present, more happens. The more faith that is present in a person, the more likely he or she will receive healing. The more faith that is being expressed in an atmosphere, the more likely it will be that waves of healing will break out among that specific group of people. Faith is important; I just never want it to become a stumbling block, preventing you from praying for a person in need.

#1: VERY WEAK FAITH: "IF YOU CAN"

The Father and His Demonized Son

> *Then one of the crowd answered and said, "Teacher, I brought You my son, who has a mute spirit. And wherever it seizes him, it throws him down; he foams at the mouth, gnashes his teeth, and becomes rigid. So I spoke to Your disciples, that they should cast it out, but they could not."*

He answered him and said, "O faithless generation, how long shall I be with you? How long shall I bear with you? Bring him to Me." Then they brought him to Him. And when he saw Him, immediately the spirit convulsed him, and he fell on the ground and wallowed, foaming at the mouth.

So He asked his father, "How long has this been happening to him?" And he said, "From childhood. And often he has thrown him both into the fire and into the water to destroy him. But if You can do anything, have compassion on us and help us."

Jesus said to him, "If you can believe, all things are possible to him who believes." Immediately the father of the child cried out and said with tears, "Lord, I believe; help my unbelief!"

When Jesus saw that the people came running together, He rebuked the unclean spirit, saying to it: "Deaf and dumb spirit, I command you, come out of him and enter him no more!" Then the spirit cried out, convulsed him greatly, and came out of him. And he became as one dead, so that many said, "He is dead." But Jesus took him by the hand and lifted him up, and he arose.

And when He had come into the house, His disciples asked Him privately, "Why could we not cast it out?" So He said to them, "This kind can come out by nothing but prayer and fasting" (Mark 9:17-29).

In verse 22, we see exactly where the father's faith level was. Consider how he responds to Jesus: *"But if You can do anything, have compassion on us and help us."* This father had an "if you can" faith level, which I would consider to be extremely low. He was not confident of an assured outcome. He was not confessing God's promises of guaranteed victory. In fact, he was struggling.

IT'S TIME FOR US TO LIFT OUR EYES AND SIMPLY VIEW GOD AS SCRIPTURE REVEALS HIM TO BE.

Very Weak Faith

The key factors that contributed to the father's low level of faith are still relevant for many of us today. First there was the seriousness of his son's condition: *"Then one of the crowd answered and said, 'Teacher, I brought You my son, who has a mute spirit. And wherever it seizes him, it throws him down; he foams at the mouth, gnashes his teeth, and becomes rigid'"* (Mark 9:17-18). You can tell how serious some people perceive their conditions to be based on how they relay their story to you. As this father spoke with Jesus, it is obvious that he considered his son's condition to be extremely serious.

This father was operating from the "if you can" mindset because he didn't know any better. We preface our prayer requests to God with "if you can" because our view of the problem is greater than our vision of the solution. This is why, first and foremost, we must have an accurate view of who God is. When we compare sickness to the greatness of God and His ability and willingness to heal, there is no contest. God is greater than any condition, no matter how serious it may appear. It's time for us to lift our eyes and simply view God as Scripture reveals Him to be.

Another factor at play here was the fact that the boy had a long-standing condition. *"So [Jesus] asked his father, 'How long has this been happening to him?' And he said, 'From childhood'"* (Mark 9:21). If someone has lived in pain for years or even decades, this can make it very difficult for them to express confidence that God will most certainly heal them. The longer the condition, the more debilitated a person's faith can become. This father had a son who had been in a very serious condition since childhood.

Another factor at play here was the fact that the disciples had failed to heal or deliver the father's son. *"So I spoke to Your disciples, that they should cast it out, but they could not"* (Mark 9:18). In "The Thrill of Victory" chapter, I shared the story about the coal miner I prayed for who, at first, wanted nothing to do with me. She already had one of Jesus' anointed modern day disciples pray for her and nothing happened.

WE WOULD DO WELL TO CREATE A LOVING, COMPASSIONATE ATMOSPHERE WHERE PEOPLE ARE FREE TO BE HONEST WITH US.

The Seed of Breakthrough in Very Weak Faith

Despite this father's very weak faith, there were seeds of breakthrough present. It is important to learn to identify the seed of breakthrough even in the most difficult of situations. This requires constant dependency upon the Holy Spirit. You need to listen for opportunities and look for open doors. Even though this father had very weak faith, he had some key factors going for him that set him and his son up for breakthrough.

First, the man was honest and did not pretend what was not true. He openly acknowledged his lack of faith. He was not even sure that Jesus *could* heal his son, let alone that He *would* heal him. He did not pretend to have faith when there was nothing. As healing ministers we would do well to create a loving, compassionate atmosphere where people are free to be honest with us.

> VERY LITTLE FAITH IS BETTER THAN
> NO FAITH AT ALL, BECAUSE AT LEAST
> YOU HAVE A SEED TO WORK WITH.

Even though this man had doubts about Jesus' ability and willingness to heal his son, he had *enough* faith to bring the child to Jesus. This is absolutely outstanding. What motivated him to bring his son to Jesus? Most likely, he was drawn by the power of testimony. Testimonies have the ability to awaken even the smallest amount of faith in an individual. This father was surely overwhelmed by the odds that were against his son, yet the fact that Jesus was healing the sick and destroying the works of the devil unlocked the very little faith this father had and drew him to Jesus. Very little faith is better than no faith at all, because at least you have a seed to work with.

In his confession of weak faith, the father also makes a powerful statement concerning the nature of Jesus: *"But if You can do anything, have compassion on us and help us"* (Mark 9:22). Compassion has the power to lower the volume of false teaching, discouragement, and strong unbelief. The person you are praying for is not simply a ministry project; the person is a suffering human being who is radically loved by God.

#2: SOME FAITH: "IF YOU ARE WILLING"

The Man with Leprosy

> *Now a leper came to Him, imploring Him, kneeling down to Him and saying to Him, "If You are willing, You can make me clean." Then Jesus, moved with compassion, stretched out His hand and touched him, and said to him, "I am willing; be cleansed." As soon as He had spoken, immediately the leprosy left him, and he was cleansed* (Mark 1:40-42).

The man with leprosy has an "if you are willing" type of faith. The "if you are willing" faith person is not necessarily questioning whether or not Jesus is *able* to heal. That issue is typically settled in their mind. They are at least beginning with a relatively high view of God's greatness, recognizing that He is God—"of course He *can* heal me. He *can* do anything." This person is coming from a strong starting point but is in need of additional encouragement when it comes to God's *willingness* to heal. It is one thing to believe that God Almighty *can* do something; it is another thing to be confident that the same God who can do all things actually *wants* to heal. People with this level of faith commonly pray, "If it would be Your will, please heal me."

IT IS ONE THING TO BELIEVE THAT GOD ALMIGHTY CAN DO SOMETHING; IT IS ANOTHER THING TO BE CONFIDENT THAT THE SAME GOD WHO CAN DO ALL THINGS ACTUALLY WANTS TO HEAL.

What Does "If You Are Willing Faith" Look and Sound Like?

In Mark 1, the leper expresses no doubt about Jesus' ability to heal. Consider the last part of the man's appeal to Jesus for healing: "You can make me clean" (Mark 1:40). There was no doubt about whether or not Jesus could heal the man. His struggle was with Jesus' willingness to heal him. The same is true for so many people today, with both believers and unbelievers.

For believers, this often comes wrapped up in "sovereignty of God" language. Sovereignty language goes something like this: "the sovereign God can do absolutely anything He wants to do, however, His will to heal someone is His sovereign choice, and His sovereign choice alone. He may be willing or He may not be willing—you just never quite know with certainty." That is sovereignty language but it is not an accurate representation of the gospel.

Jesus dispels this idea entirely with every healing He performs. Perhaps one of the greatest indicators of God's willingness to heal everyone is seen in how Jesus responds to this man with leprosy. After the man affirms Jesus' ability to heal, Jesus turns around and confirms His willingness to heal: "Then Jesus, moved with compassion, stretched out His hand and touched him, and said to him, 'I am willing; be cleansed'" (Mark 1:41).

DESPERATION HAS THE ABILITY TO OVERRIDE THEOLOGY AND BRING A PERSON INTO A DIVINE ENCOUNTER WITH GOD'S HEALING POWER.

What Supported the Leper's "If You Are Willing" Faith?

The leper was not offering Jesus a casual request for healing. Even though he used the "if it be Your will" language, He was nevertheless begging Jesus, *imploring Him* to heal his condition. Desperation has the ability to override theology and bring a person into a divine encounter with God's healing power. When we pray for people, we are not ministering to their deficiency or lack, but rather we are calling forth whatever seeds of faith they are exhibiting. In both the person with a weak expression of faith and the one with some measure of faith, it is amazing how powerful is the simple act of coming to Jesus. When people see us, they should see Jesus. They should hear Him calling them to come. They should sense His compassion in us as ambassadors of Christ.

Lastly, like the father with the tormented son, there is good reason to believe that the man with leprosy came to Jesus because he heard the testimony of what Jesus was doing.

Tell Them "I Am Willing!"

In the gospel of Mark, we see once again that Jesus does not turn the leper away. He does not rebuke him for not having an abundance of faith. Moved with compassion, Jesus responds simply but profoundly: *"I am willing"* (Mark 1:41). Jesus takes delight in revealing His willingness to those who have an understanding of His ability. This is a powerful truth and when it is infused with a person's belief, faith for healing can rise in their heart. If the God who created the heavens and the earth is willing to heal me, how in the world could I second-guess Him? There is truly nothing impossible for Him!

IF THE GOD WHO CREATED THE HEAVENS AND
THE EARTH IS WILLING TO HEAL ME, HOW IN
THE WORLD COULD I SECOND-GUESS HIM?

When you pray for those who have "if you are willing" faith, lovingly encourage them that the Jesus who *can* is also *willing*. I believe the Holy Spirit is crying out, "Tell them I am willing!" Just as Jesus boldly made this statement to the leper, you, as Jesus' representative, should be sharing the same truth.

#3: GREAT FAITH: "IF I CAN"

The Woman with the Issue of Blood

> *Now a certain woman had a flow of blood for twelve years, and had suffered many things from many physicians. She had spent all that she had and was no better, but rather grew worse. When she heard about Jesus, she came behind Him in the crowd and touched His garment. For she said, "If only I may touch His clothes, I shall be made well."*
>
> *Immediately the fountain of her blood was dried up, and she felt in her body that she was healed of the affliction. And Jesus, immediately knowing in Himself that power had gone out of Him, turned around in the crowd and said, "Who touched My clothes?"*
>
> *But His disciples said to Him, "You see the multitude thronging You, and You say, 'Who touched Me?'" And He looked around to see her who had done this thing. But the woman, fearing and trembling, knowing what had happened to her, came and fell down before Him and told Him the whole truth. And He said to her, "Daughter, your faith has made you well. Go in peace, and be healed of your affliction"* (Mark 5:25-34 NKJV).

This is one of the most well known stories of healing in the gospels. We have looked at this scripture earlier, but I am using it again here because it is an excellent example of great faith. To understand the magnitude of her healing, consider the following observations about the woman's unique infirmity. First, the constant flow of blood made her a social outcast by religious tradition. She was most likely ostracized and rejected by the "community of faith" at the time.

Second, her condition was a long-standing condition, lasting twelve years (see Mark 5:25). Just imagine how this could have impacted her faith. If any person had reason to give up on the possibility of being healed, it was this woman. However, she still had faith to receive her healing after twelve years.

AFFLICTION IS COSTLY.

Third, this woman had suffered a great deal from her condition (see Mark 5:26). Her suffering was holistic—there was great pain and tremendous shame. This was not a minor condition.

Fourth, she had been to many doctors and none were able to provide relief (see Mark 5:26). She had every right in the natural to give up hope for healing. There came a point when the medical science of her day could not help her. This is true for many today who suffer from certain diseases and afflictions. This is by no means intended to discourage people from visiting doctors or receiving medical treatment. Instead, we can encourage them that there is more—and His name is Jesus, the One who heals.

Fifth, this woman spent all of her money trying to get healed (see Mark 5:26). Affliction is costly. She did everything possible to invest in her healing in the natural. Unfortunately, none of the investments paid off.

What Does "If I Can" Faith Look and Sound Like?

Having just reviewed those things that were coming against this woman and her faith, let's look at how she responded.

A PERSON'S LEVEL OF RISK TENDS TO
CORRESPOND WITH THEIR LEVEL OF FAITH.

First, this woman approached Jesus with knowledge of who He was and what He had done: *"When she heard about Jesus, she came behind Him in the crowd..."* (Mark 5:27). Testimony most likely played a part. It is likely that these testimonies reoriented her perspective. There is a strong possibility that before she was introduced to Jesus through these stories, she was on the verge of giving up. Then, everything changed when she heard about Jesus. Suddenly she was just focused on getting to Jesus. As she pressed through the crowd, we get to hear her faith. *She kept saying, If I only touch His garments, I shall be restored to health"* (Mark 5:28 AMP).

Second, she approached Jesus with disregard for her religious tradition that required her to stay out of public—especially away from holy people. That is "if I can" faith in action and it is often spelled r-i-s-k. She took a tremendous risk, including the possibility of stoning, when she approached Jesus. People who have very weak faith or some faith will not take extreme risks like this. A person's level of risk tends to correspond with their level of faith. In essence, she was saying that she would rather die for pressing into Jesus, in hope, than go on living hopeless and defeated in her condition. This kind of tenacity is the birthplace for significant healings and miracles.

Fourth, the woman pressed through the crowd with persistence and determination. When someone has an accurate view of Jesus—who He is, what He is able to do, and what He is willing to do—they cannot remain stationary. Even though there are obstacles to be overcome, staying in the place of defeat is no longer an option. This is precisely what happened to this woman. Motivated by the testimony of Jesus, she pressed through the obstacles and touched the One who changed everything.

TENACITY IS THE BIRTHPLACE FOR
SIGNIFICANT HEALINGS AND MIRACLES.

What Happened to the Woman because of Her "If I Can" Faith?

The woman with the issue of blood positioned herself to get healed. This is a key quality of "if I can" faith. There is an emphasis on "I" for one reason—you and I often have something to say about our healing. We can either position ourselves to receive healing, or we can remain in the place of doubt, unbelief, pain, and discouragement. I am not promising instant results in every situation. Remember, healing is always God's responsibility. The Bible confirms that God is willing. However, the *where* and *when* of how the healing manifests is in God's capable, loving hands.

We should not be preoccupied with the mechanics of how healing might take place. This woman was certainly not focused on such things. In fact, when you read the story, it seems as if she was "making it up as she went!" As she pressed through the crowd, I am sure she wondered—moment by moment—"When are they going to find me out and what will they do to me when they find me?" Fear will always target your faith. This is why you need to recognize that faith does not mean an absence of fear. Instead, faith means taking risks based on God's Word instead of catering to fear.

Because of this incredible risk, the woman was immediately healed. Her demonstration of faith brought instant physical results. She could feel in her body that she was healed, as *"immediately the fountain of her blood was dried up, and she felt in her body that she was healed of the affliction"* (Mark 5:29).

FEAR WILL ALWAYS TARGET YOUR FAITH.
FAITH DOES NOT MEAN AN ABSENCE OF FEAR.
FAITH MEANS TAKING RISKS BASED ON GOD'S
WORD INSTEAD OF CATERING TO FEAR.

When you notice this kind of faith in the person you are praying for, be greatly encouraged. I am not saying that you will experience this sort of *instant healing* scenario every single time you encounter a person with this type of faith.

However, know that when someone expresses this "if I can" kind of faith, they have positioned themselves for the possibility of an instant, immediate, miraculous healing.

#4: RECKLESS FAITH: "I CAN'T, BUT HE CAN"

Blind Bartimaeus

> *Now they came to Jericho. As He went out of Jericho with His disciples and a great multitude, blind Barti-maeus, the son of Timaeus, sat by the road begging. And when he heard that it was Jesus of Nazareth, he began to cry out and say, "Jesus, Son of David, have mercy on me!"*
>
> *Then many warned him to be quiet; but he cried out all the more, "Son of David, have mercy on me!" So Jesus stood still and commanded him to be called. Then they called the blind man, saying to him, "Be of good cheer. Rise, He is calling you." And throwing aside his garment, he rose and came to Jesus.*
>
> *So Jesus answered and said to him, "What do you want Me to do for you?" The blind man said to Him, "Rabboni, that I may receive my sight." Then Jesus said to him, "Go your way; your faith has made you well." And immediately he received his sight and followed Jesus on the road* (Mark 10:46-52).

The Blind Man's Condition

In my opinion blind Barttimaeus demonstrates the greatest faith of anyone in these four stories. He does not have the ability to touch Jesus or even to find his way to Jesus. All he has is hope. I can just imagine him, having heard of Jesus, sitting there day after day, hoping he might just be in the right place at the right time—when Jesus passes by.

The Response of Reckless Faith

When Bartimaeus heard that Jesus was passing by, he yelled out, "Jesus, Son of David, have mercy on me! Jesus, Son of David, have mercy on me!" He was not timid or tame in his expression of faith. His shout revealed his respect of and faith in Jesus as the Messiah, when he acknowledged Him as "Son of David."

Some in the crowd went over to him and rebuked him. "Shhh! Be still," they cried. But he yelled out all the more, "Jesus, Son of David, have mercy on me!" Persistence was instrumental in positioning this blind beggar for healing. When the crowd tried to quiet him down, his cries got louder!

He kept crying out because he recognized the limited opportunity before him. He knew that his voice must be heard before Jesus passed by or his chance for healing would be gone. He had only a few, brief minutes. He had to shout because there were so many people around Jesus. What motivated Bartimaeus to cry out so loudly? How did he know that the Son of David could heal and desired to heal a blind beggar? I believe it was testimony that gave Bartimaeus faith that Jesus would heal him. He had heard that Jesus of Nazareth was coming and this news was of value to him because he had heard the testimonies of Jesus' healing power.

How Jesus Responded to Reckless Faith

Jesus heard the cries of Bartimaues and said, "Call him." Right here, we see a very important lesson in healing. A message ushered in his healing. A messenger told blind Bartimaeus, *"The Master is calling you!"* Whoever gave Bartimaeus this message was, in essence, sharing a word of knowledge with him.

As soon as Bartimaeus received this message, he got up and threw off his cloak. This is a significant nuance of the story that we cannot overlook because it was a bold act of faith. This was an official cloak given to him by the religious officials that signified he was a legitimate beggar worthy of receiving alms. When he took it off and threw in on the ground he was declaring that he was no longer blind. With that one gesture, he announced to the world, "I don't need this cloak anymore!" All of this took place, before he was healed.

Bartimaeus responded to Jesus and came to Him, and it was then that Jesus asked a seemingly strange question. He said, "What do you want Me to do for you?" This is a very important question, because it can determine what people receive from God and whether or not they get healed. Think about it. Perhaps you will encounter someone who is blind. You ask them, "What do you want God to do for you?" Maybe they answer, "Increase my patience," or "Help me to be a good missionary, even though I am blind." They are asking for noble things, certainly, but they are not addressing the central issue of blindness. They are not confronting their condition. Bartimaeus specifically said, "Rabbi, I want to see," and Jesus healed him.

Whether you encounter someone with weak faith, willing faith or strong faith, once you understand their level of faith you will have greater clarity and confidence to pray for their healing.

INTO THE FLOW OF GRACE

THE CENTRALITY OF GOD'S PRESENCE IN HEALING

We end our journey into the ministry of healing in the same place that we started, in the presence of God. If you are called to the ministry of healing, it is vitally important that you learn how to stand in the flow of grace coming from the throne of God. You and I do not have the power to heal in and of ourselves. When we start thinking that healing is our responsibility, we actually step out of the flow of grace. It does not matter who stewards the gift or carries the anointing, only One has the power to heal, and that is the Lord Jesus Christ. He *will* anoint you with His Spirit to continue this ministry if you ask Him.

When I was ministering at a church in Raleigh, North Carolina, some time ago, a cloud of God's glory like a pillar appeared in the meeting. You could see red, silver and gold swirling in this glory cloud. A lot of peace and a lot of healing took place in the presence of this glory cloud. When we began to pray, we found that on the side of the church where the glory cloud appeared, three or four times as many people got healed as were healed on the other side of the church. The only difference was how close the people were to the cloud. There was an older man there who was deaf from his time in the Korean War. No one prayed for him. He just happened to be sitting right in front of the cloud, and after fifty years of deafness, he was healed. Why? Because he was close to the glory of God!

WHEN WE START THINKING THAT HEALING IS OUR RESPONSIBILITY, WE ACTUALLY STEP OUT OF THE FLOW OF GRACE.

Once, Heidi Baker was ministering in northern Mozambique, in a Muslim area, and the glory cloud came. Around the perimeter of the meeting there were people who were mocking her—witch doctors, Muslim clerics, and other Muslims. They were making fun and mocking, and then the glory cloud came. This cloud was so bright that the speaker could not see to read. Everyone fell to the ground. When the cloud lifted, there was not one sick person in their midst. Every single person had been healed without anyone praying for anything. In addition, there were no more unbelievers, no witch doctors, and no Muslim clerics left because everybody now believed in Jesus Christ. It was supernatural and sovereign healing and it brought unbelievers to Christ.

A former leader of the Assemblies of God told me that after God's power broke out in Pensacola, some men came to the church, and they caught the anointing. These men then carried this anointing to another church that evening, and, as the glory came, people were healed of everything. No one prayed. The healings that happened that night were sovereign. This is what happens when God's presence manifests in great power. This same power resides within you. The same God who manifests in glory clouds, causing mass salvations and healings lives inside of you. He longs to use you to touch others, to release them from the grip of disease and death, to set the captives free.

In 2 Samuel 22:13 David sings songs of praise to God for delivering him from the hands of his enemies.

> *"I call to the Lord who is worthy of praise, and I am saved from my enemies."* (2 Samuel 22:4)

But David doesn't stop there. He is a man after God's own heart and in spite of many obstacles he continues to press into the presence of God.

> *". . . you fill me with joy in your presence, with eternal pleasures at your right hand."* (Psalm 16:11)

> *"Where can I go from your Spirit? Where can I flee from your presence? If I go up to the heavens, you are there; if I make my bed in the depths, you are there. If I rise on the wings of the dawn, if I settle on the far*

side of the sea, even there your hand will guide me."
(Psalm 139:7-10)

God is with us! His glorious presence was made manifest in a humble manger. He came and lived among us as a man, because He loves us. He sacrificed His only Son on the cross, forever removing the barrier that separated God and man, so that not one will perish. By His stripes we are healed!

It is my hope that you will find this book to be a very practical guidebook for the ministry of healing. It is a great desire of my heart to see every believer operating in the ministry of healing that is available to us all because healing brings glory to God. Study the principles presented in this book, but never forget that the greatest principle is to be grounded in the reality of *God's presence above everything else.* Be open, yield to the Holy Spirit, and treasure God's presence because He is the King of endless glory! Plant your feet firmly in the flow of His grace and watch miracles, signs and wonders flow from the Throne. Trust Him even when you do not see His power manifest. The responsibility for healing belongs to God and to Him alone. I love this beautiful doxology found at the end of the Book of Jude.

To him who is able to keep you from falling and to present you before his glorious presence without fault and with great joy—to the only God our Savior be glory, majesty, power and authority, through Jesus Christ our Lord, before all ages, now and forevermore! Amen. (Jude 1:24 NIV)

WATCH GOD ACCOMPLISH THE MIRACULOUS

THROUGH YOU.

LEARN FROM DR. RANDY CLARK!

Every Christian has been sent and empowered by Jesus to heal the sick. The problem is that many of us don't know how to practically complete this task.

In the *Power to Heal* curriculum, international evangelist, teacher, and apostolic voice, Dr. Randy Clark, shares eight practical, Bible-based tools that will help you start praying for the sick and see them supernaturally healed!

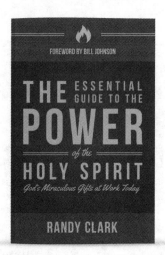

Christian Prophetic
CERTIFICATION PROGRAM

We are happy to announce the launch of the
**Christian Prophetic Certification Program
(CPCP).**

CPCP will teach students how to recognize the gift of prophecy in their own life, allowing them to better recognize communications from the Holy Spirit.

Students will gain a truly Biblical perspective on the prophetic both from the Old and New Testaments. They will also learn about the history of prophesy within the church, its benefits and the ways in which it went off track.

**Courses are available online
and can be taken anywhere at any time.**

Check out our website for more details at
propheticcertification.com

JOIN US!

globalawakening

lighting fires • building bridges • casting vision

Based in Mechanicsburg, PA, the Apostolic Network of Global Awakening (ANGA) is a teaching, healing and impartation ministry with a heart for the nations. Founded in 1994 by Randy Clark after his involvement with the Toronto Airport Christian Fellowship revival, the ministry exists to fulfill the biblical commissions of Jesus:

> *As you go preach, saying the Kingdom of heaven is at hand. Heal the sick, cleanse the lepers, raise the dead, cast out demons. Freely you have received, freely give (Matthew 10:7-8).*

> *Therefore go and make disciples of all nations, baptizing them in the name of the Father and of the Son and of the Holy Spirit, and teaching them to obey everything I have commanded you. And surely I am with you always, to the very end of the age (Matthew 28:19-20).*

Through the formation of ANGA, International Ministry Trips (IMT), the Schools of Healing and Impartation and the Global School of Supernatural Ministry, Global Awakening offers training, conferences, humanitarian aid, and ministry trips in an effort to raise up a company of men and women who will facilitate revival among the nation's leaders. By providing an assortment of international training opportunities, the ministry works in accordance with the revelation to the Apostle Paul regarding the purpose of the five fold ministries:

> *It was He who gave some to be apostles, some to be prophets, some to be evangelists, and some to be pastors and teachers, to prepare God's people for works of service, so that the body of Christ may be built up until we all reach unity in the faith and in the knowledge of the Son of God and become mature, attaining to the whole measure of the fullness of Christ (Ephesians 4:11-13).*

Led by Dr. Randy Clark, the ministry has visited over 36 countries and continues to travel extensively to bring hope, healing, and power to the nations.

globalawakening.com

f ▶️ 🐦 📷 🔊

Purdchase all of Dr. Randy Clark's books at:
globalawakeningstore.com

LEARN TO MINISTER AS JESUS DID.

"Christian Healing Certification Program is sure to help people come into a greater understanding of this vital area of ministry. And even more important is that participants will have greater fruitfulness for the glory of God. I highly recommend this training program. It will change your life."

-BILL JOHNSON, BETHEL CHURCH, REDDING, CA

Do you feel a stirring in your heart to take the next step in preparation for ministry? Do you want to see healing and deliverance operating in your own life? Join us for one of our online classes in the areas of Physical Healing, Deliverance or Inner Healing.

No Prior training necessary

Courses are available to fit your schedule

Small and personal classes of 15-17 students per class

It's easy and can be done right from home

Economical and inexpensive

Join a community of online students from all over the world

Over one thousand people have completed coursework

For more information or to register, visit our website at **www.healingcertification.com** or call **717.796.9866 X124**. Most materials avaiable at global Awakening Bookstore.

Christian Healing
CERTIFICATION PROGRAM